How to Transfer Your Skills
in Desktop Publishing Software

Lea Weston

PITMAN PUBLISHING
128 Long Acre, London WC2E 9AN

A Division of Longman Group UK Limited

© Lea Weston 1993

First published in Great Britain 1993

British Library Cataloguing in Publication Data
A catalogue record for this book is available from the British Library

ISBN 0273 03936 9

Printed in England by Clays Ltd, St Ives plc

Contents ▬▬▬▬▬▬

Contents

Preface

Desktop Publishing (DTP) arrived in 1985 with the Apple MacIntosh and Aldus PageMaker. Even though Apple retains a strong hold within the graphic design profession, the PC is fast becoming a reasonable alternative for professional design studios.

Desktop Publishing is the ability to produce a document which gives the appearance of having been set up in printers type using a conventional typesetting machine. Documents with impressive layouts and incorporating photographs, graphics and a multitude of typefaces can be produced - all without a degree in typography or a lifetime's experience in the printing industry.

The top end of the DTP market for PC's is dominated by Ventura Publisher and Aldus PageMaker. Ventura is renowned for its ability to handle long documents and cope with intricacies such as indexing and cross-referencing while PageMaker is more flexible and easier to learn. The budget end of the market is dominated by Timeworks Publisher which has a Ventura-like appearance.

Ventura Publisher is probably the best DTP package for books and manuals while PageMaker's flexibility in positioning text makes it better suited to magazine layout.

This guide looks at three Desktop Publishing packages and compares the way in which basic functions are handled in each. It explains in simple terms the functions of each system and will enable an operator to move easily and quickly from one package to another.

Part 1: Conversion Guide
This section takes you through the transition from one package to another: Ventura GEM to Ventura Windows, Ventura GEM to PageMaker, and Timeworks Publisher to PageMaker. It also includes advice on planning your publication and an outline of the steps involved in production.

Part 2: Quick Reference

This section covers each software application giving you concise instructions on how to carry out the most basic and necessary functions.

The **Appendix** includes a useful listing of the function keys and the keyboard conventions for each program, Hints and Tips on operating a Desktop Publising system and a glossary of DTP terms.

Part 1
Conversion Guide

━━━

The Windows environment is here to stay. This is verified not only by the computer press but also by the number of Microsoft Windows3 users worldwide. Because of this the Desktop Publishing world is developing in the same direction.

Since its inception Ventura has used the GEM environment from Digital Research. Recently however, Ventura issued both a Windows and a Mac version of its Desktop Publishing program. Already the support for font managers and device drivers makes Windows a much better environment than GEM.

PageMaker has been meeting Desktop Publication requirements for as long as Ventura. Whereas Ventura takes a chapter/frame appproach to the construction of a publication, however in PageMaker the central concept is that of the page. One of the main practical differences between the frame-based and non-frame based approaches is that you can override text placement between columns in a non-frame based program.

Whichever package you use, always remember the golden rule:
Plan your publication before you start.

Ventura GEM to Ventura Windows

The step from Ventura GEM to Ventura Windows is not as drastic as the change from one application to another. The basic program setup is still the same but the Ventura Publisher 4.0 for Windows version has integrated previously unavailable features.

The new features in Windows include: search and replace, spell check, undo/redo, object linking and embedding (OLE) and support for Word for Windows 2.0. Also new in Ventura 4 for Windows is the 24 bit colour support which includes Pantone's 700 spot colour. (This guide does not cover this advanced technique, although it is available for the professional user.)

The new search and replace facility is very powerful: you may search and replace not only text but fonts, tags and text attributes.

One of the main differences between the GEM and Windows versions is the screen layout and menu structures. These are illustrated in full in the Ventura Publisher Quick Reference section and in part on the following two pages.

While the software differences are minimal, where these two products really do vary is in their hardware requirements. The GEM version can be run on an XT, although it will perform better on a 286 or above. Ventura Publisher for Windows however, requires the Windows 3 environment and performs better with a 386/33 with minimum 4mb RAM.

Once you have mastered the altered screen layout, menu structure and minor keyboard shortcut changes you will soon adapt to Ventura Publisher for Windows.

Ventura GEM toolbox definitions

+	**Frame Mode** to draw, resize and move frames as well as import text	**Ctrl U**
≡	**Paragraph Mode** to work with entire paragraphs of text using paragraph styles	**Ctrl I**
Y	**Text Mode** to type, edit and restyle text	**Ctrl O**
↑	**Graphics Mode** to draw simple graphics such as lines, circles and rectangles	**Ctrl P**

GEM Graphics toolbox

\	Straight line tool	⬭	Rounded corners tool
☐	Rectangle tool	○	Circle tool
↑	Pointer tool	Box Text	Similar to a regular frame but can only be on column

GEM Graphics cursor shapes

— Line

⌐ Rectangle

⊕ Circle

⌐ Rounded rectangle

Ventura Windows toolbox

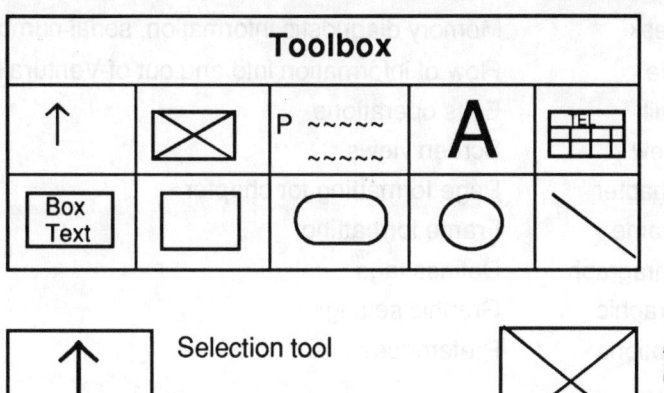

Toolbox				

Selection tool

Add New Frame tool
Ctrl U

Paragraph tool
Ctrl I

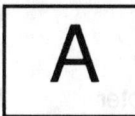
Text tool
Ctrl O

Table tool
Ctrl P

Graphics tools

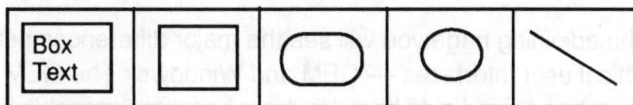

Box text tool
Rectangle tool
Rounded rectangle tool
Circle tool
Line tool

Ventura Gem to Ventura Windows menu comparisons _____

Ventura Gem

Desk	Memory diagnostic information, serial number
File	Flow of information into and out of Ventura Publisher
Edit	Edits operations
View	Screen views
Chapter	Page formatting for chapter
Frame	Frame formatting
Paragraph	Defines tags
Graphic	Graphic settings
Options	Preferences

Ventura Windows

File	Flow of information into and out of Ventura Publisher
Edit	Edits operations
View	Screen views
Chapter	Page formatting for chapter
Frame	Frame formatting
Paragraph	Defines tags
Text	Insert and text attributes
Graphic	Graphic settings
Table	Insert and edit tables
Help	Comprehensive on-line help

Ventura GEM to Ventura Windows screen comparisons _____

On the adjoining page you will see the major differences between the two graphical user interfaces — GEM and Windows. The GEM screen layout for Ventura has a fixed side bar; Windows has three movable windows: Toolbox, Tags and Files which can be placed anywhere in the work area. It means that you don't have to display them on the screen all the time.

The Windows screen layout on the opposite page shows the entry screen without the additional windows. To see the screen with these displayed refer to page 79 in the Quick Reference Guide.

Ventura GEM screen layout _____

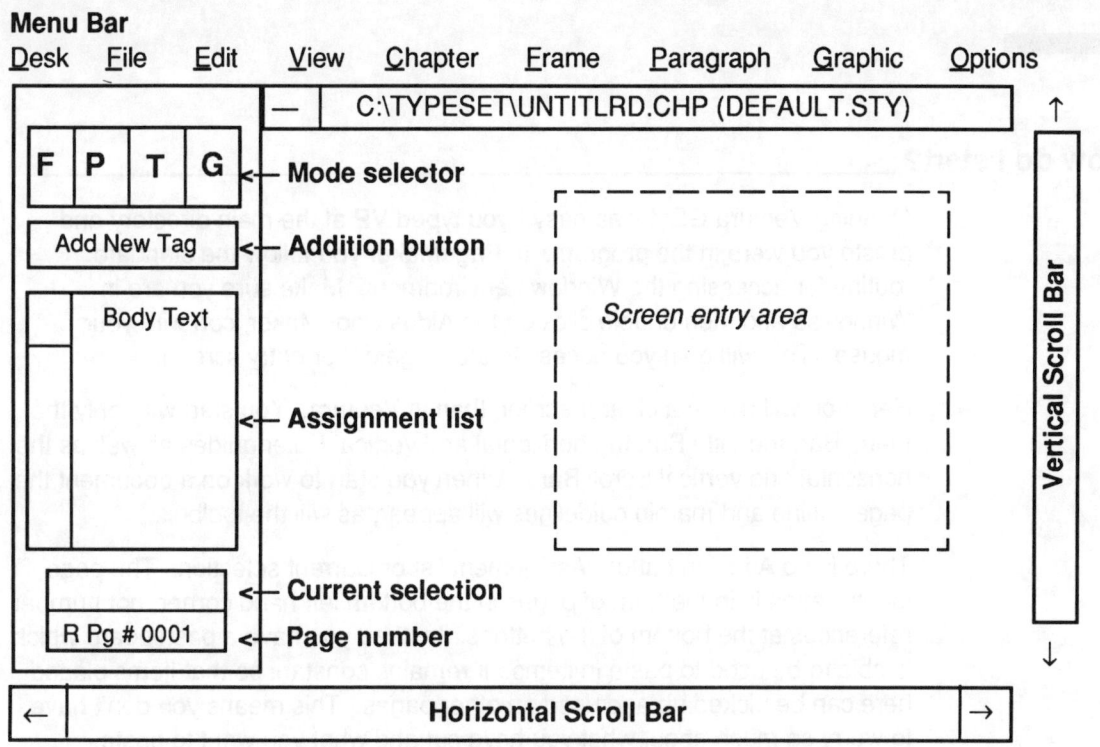

Ventura Windows screen layout _____

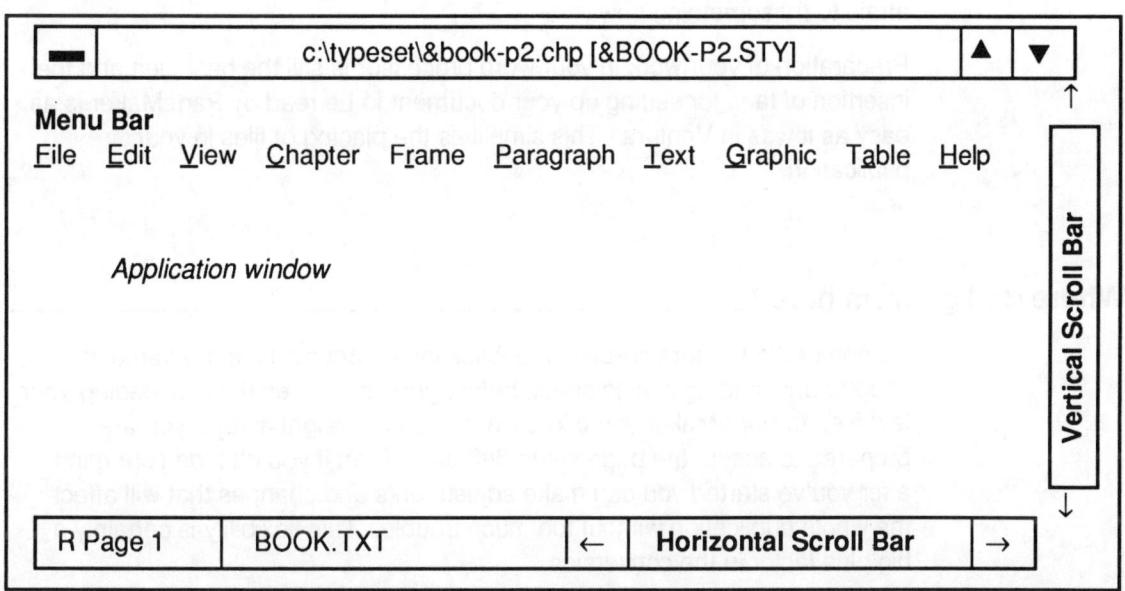

Ventura to PageMaker

How do I start?

Opening Ventura GEM was easy - you typed **VP** at the main directory and presto you were in the program. In PageMaker you follow the standard routine for accessing the Windows environment. Make sure you are in Windows3 and then double click on the Aldus PageMaker icon with your mouse. This will gain you access to the PageMaker entry screen.

Here you will notice a clearer screen than in Ventura. You start with only the Menu Bar, the Title Bar, the horizontal and vertical Ruler guides as well as the horizontal and vertical Scroll Bars. When you start to work on a document the page outline and margin guidelines will appear, as will the toolbox.

There is no Addition button, Assignment list or Current selection. The page identification is in the form of pages in the bottom left hand corner, not number references at the bottom of the buttons. Instead you have a pasteboard which is able to be used to paste in items. It remains constant so that items placed here can be picked up and used on other pages. This means you don't have to worry so much about what you have cut and what you want to paste.

You are ready to start working on your publication. The principles you learned when you first started using a computer still apply: you must save your work regularly, you must plan your ideas before you start, and you must not be afraid to try something new.

Preparation of your work in your word processor is still the best idea and the insertion of tags for setting up your document to be read by PageMaker is as easy as it was in Ventura. This simplifies the placing of files in your publication.

Where do I go from here?

Remember in Ventura creating a publication meant defining the frame, the chapter and loading a style sheet, before you could even think of loading your text file. In PageMaker you could virtually start straight away if you are prepared to accept the page setup defaults. Even if you change your mind after you've started you can make adjustments and changes that will affect the whole publication without too much trouble. This flexibility is certainly a big plus factor in the conversion.

For example you've prepared your document with the default Body Text style of Times Roman 10 point and you decide you want it to be Palatino 11 point. Select **Type menu**, **Define styles**, **Body text**, **Edit** and make the necessary changes. When you click **OK** to accept the change to body text the whole document changes to the new body text style. As easy as that.

Another bonus point in PageMaker is the word-processing facility available through the **Story Editor** which allows you to spell check or search and replace text in your publication. This means that direct text input is easy and saves having to go back to your wordprocessor to make amendments there and then re-import your story. The other difference on direct text input is that you can type text anywhere on the page. Direct text input in Ventura is always at the start of the page. PageMaker will accept direct text input where you want it and you can move the text block to where you want it also.

How do I perform the basic functions?

With the two packages so different in their conception and setup it is a bit difficult comparing the basic functions. However, below is a list of the main functions and access items that you may need. You will see PageMaker has more keyboard speed keys than Ventura and this helps reduce the access time to the menus, and is easier to use for keyboard operators.

Item	Ventura	PageMaker
New document	-	Ctrl N
Open document	-	Ctrl O
Print document	-	Ctrl P
Save document	Ctrl S	Ctrl S
Place file	-	Ctrl D
GoTo	Ctrl G	Ctrl G
Indents/tabs	-	Ctrl I
Type specifications	-	Ctrl T
Search & replace	Not available	Ctrl E Ctrl 9
Spell check	Not available	Ctrl E Ctrl L
View page:		
Fit in window	Ctrl R	Ctrl W
Actual size	Ctrl N	Ctrl 1
200%	Ctrl E	Ctrl 2
Exit	-	Ctrl Q

Creating a publication — Ventura flowchart _____

The following flow charts show the subtle differences in the decison making process of creating a document. In Ventura you will note that there are more steps to follow before you actually start on your publication.

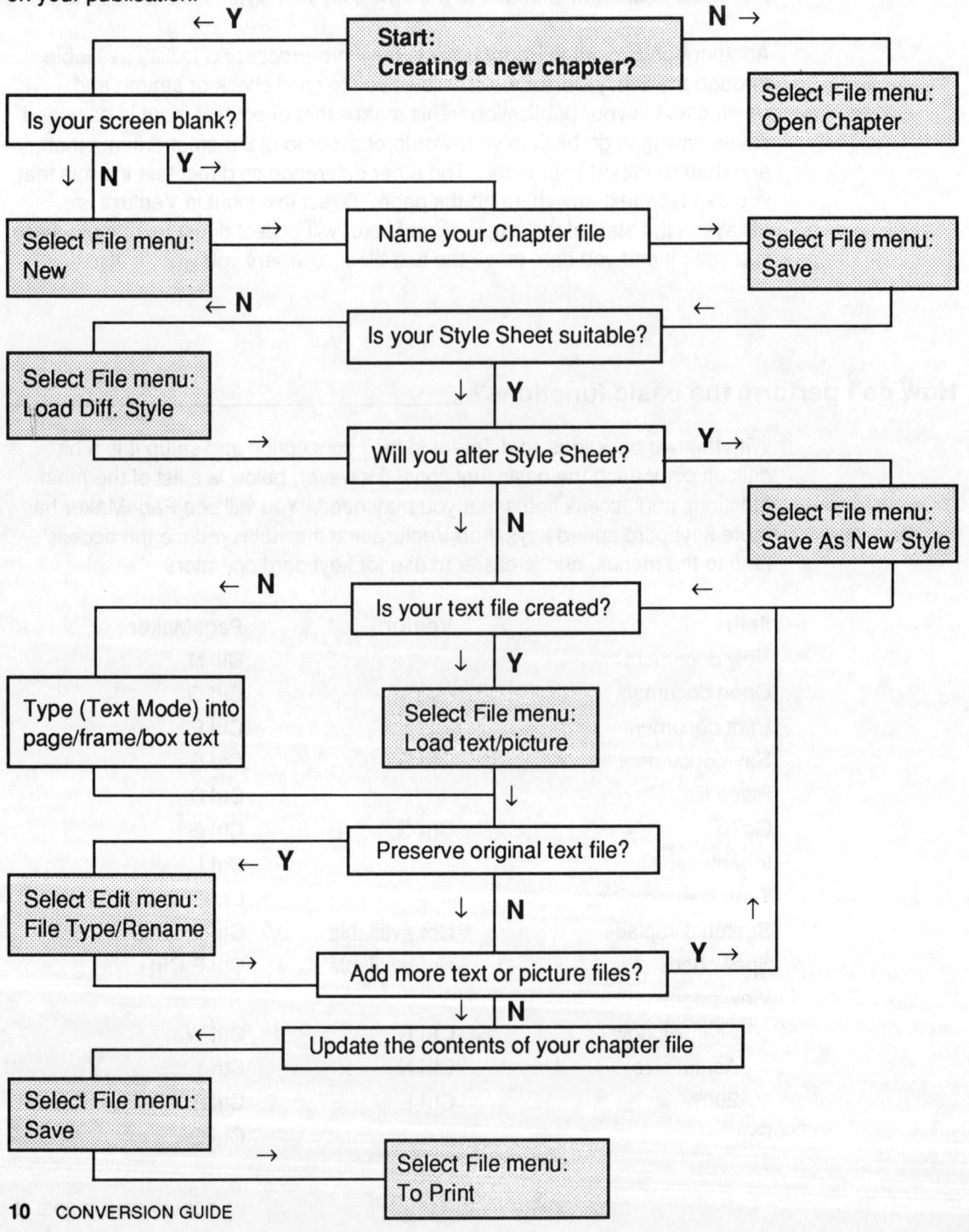

Creating a publication — PageMaker flowchart _____

This flow chart outlines the steps in creating a new publication in PageMaker. You will notice that you are able to start straight into a document with either the File New command or the File Open command.

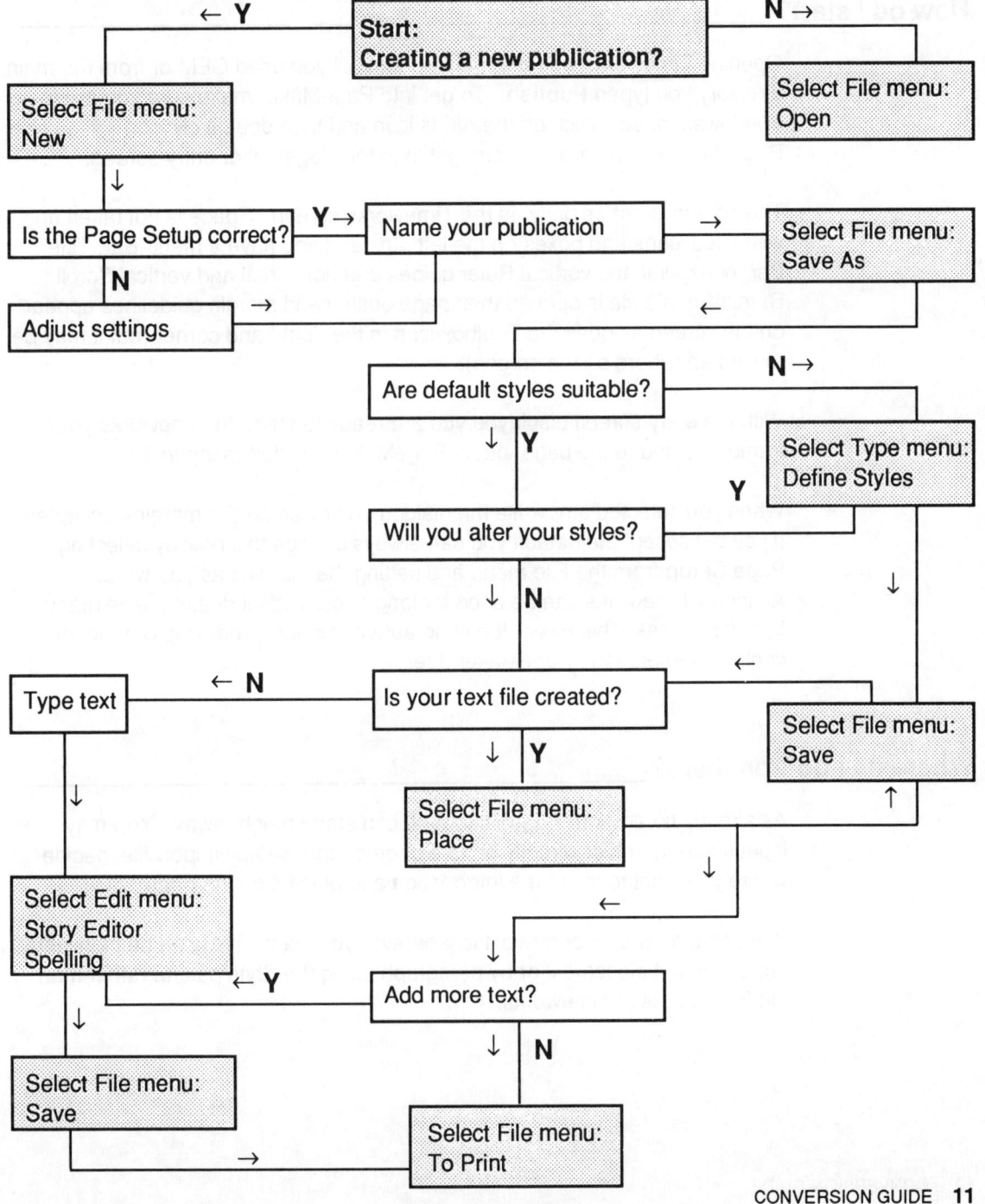

Timeworks Publisher to PageMaker

How do I start?

Opening Timeworks was a three step move if you used GEM or from the main directory you typed **Publish**. To get into PageMaker make sure you are in Windows3, double click on the Aldus icon and then double click on PageMaker4. You are then straight in to the PageMaker entry screen.

The screen is not as busy as the Timeworks screen. Space is not taken up with fixed icons and boxes on the left. Instead you have a Menu Bar, Title Bar, horizontal and vertical Ruler guides and horizontal and vertical Scroll Bars. When a file is opened then page outline and margin guidelines appear on the screen as does the Toolbox icon in the right hand corner (but it may be moved anywhere on the screen).

With the entry screen displayed you are ready to start. In Timeworks your frame was tied to the page, but in PageMaker it is tied to the text.

When you selected a new file the dialogue box wanted the margins accepted. If you did accept the default you can always change this now by selecting **Page Setup** from the File menu and setting the margins as you want. Although Timeworks can be used for long documents it doesn't have many facilities to make this easy. It has no auto numbering, indexing or table of contents generation. PageMaker does.

Where do I go from here?

As already noted, with PageMaker you can start straight away. You may input text or graphics directly on to a page or choose any import file, decide where you want to insert the information and place it on the page.

You can then drag it or move it to wherever you want. Text can be highlighted and amended piecemeal or by paragraph using the Style palette rather than the Browser as in Timeworks.

The Style Editor in PageMaker is a wordprocessing facility that is not available in Timeworks. It offers the added benefit of a spell check which means text typed in PageMaker can be reviewed for mistakes before completion of your publication.

The Master Page setup is similar in Timeworks and PageMaker. You can set the page layout, draw lines and boxes, include footers and headers and define the master setup for your publication. It is not, however, a rigid setup. In PageMaker you can toggle master page layout by selecting **Display master layout** from the Page menu. This allows you to display the master layout and change the master page settings. A different setting on an individual page automatically over-rides master page settings.

How do I perform the basic functions? _____

One of the major differences between Timeworks and PageMaker is the frames idea. Timeworks has frames, PageMaker does not. The point and stick principle of PageMaker suits the vast majority of office users who have no previous publishing experience.

Both Timeworks and PageMaker make adequate use of keyboard commands and they compare as follows:

Item	Timeworks	PageMaker
New document	-	Ctrl N
Open document	Alt O	Ctrl O
Print document	Alt P	Ctrl P
Save document	Alt S	Ctrl S
Place file	-	Ctrl D
GoTo	Alt G	Ctrl G
Indents/tabs	-	Ctrl I
Type specifications	Alt T	Ctrl T
Search & replace	Alt R	Ctrl E Ctrl 9
Spell check	Not available	Ctrl E Ctrl L
View page:		
Fit in window	Alt 4	Ctrl W
Actual size	Alt 2	Ctrl 1
200%	Alt 3	Ctrl 2
Exit	Alt Q	Ctrl Q

Creating a publication - Timeworks Publisher flowchart _____

The following flow charts show the subtle differences in the decision making process of creating a document. In Timeworks the major difference is the **Draw Frames** box.

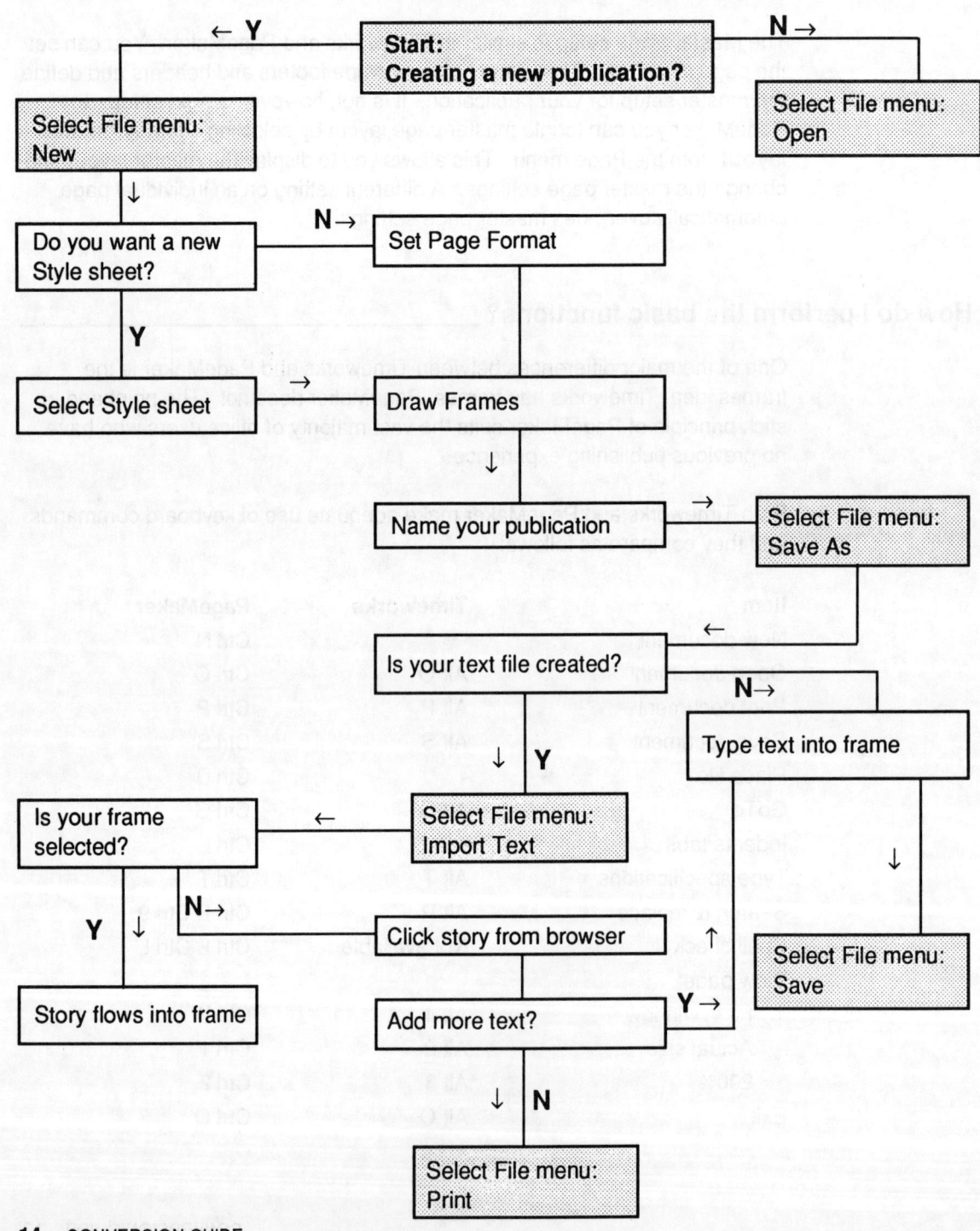

Creating a publication - PageMaker flowchart

This flow chart outlines the steps in creating a new publication in PageMaker. You will notice that you are able to start straight into a document with either the File New command or the File Open command.

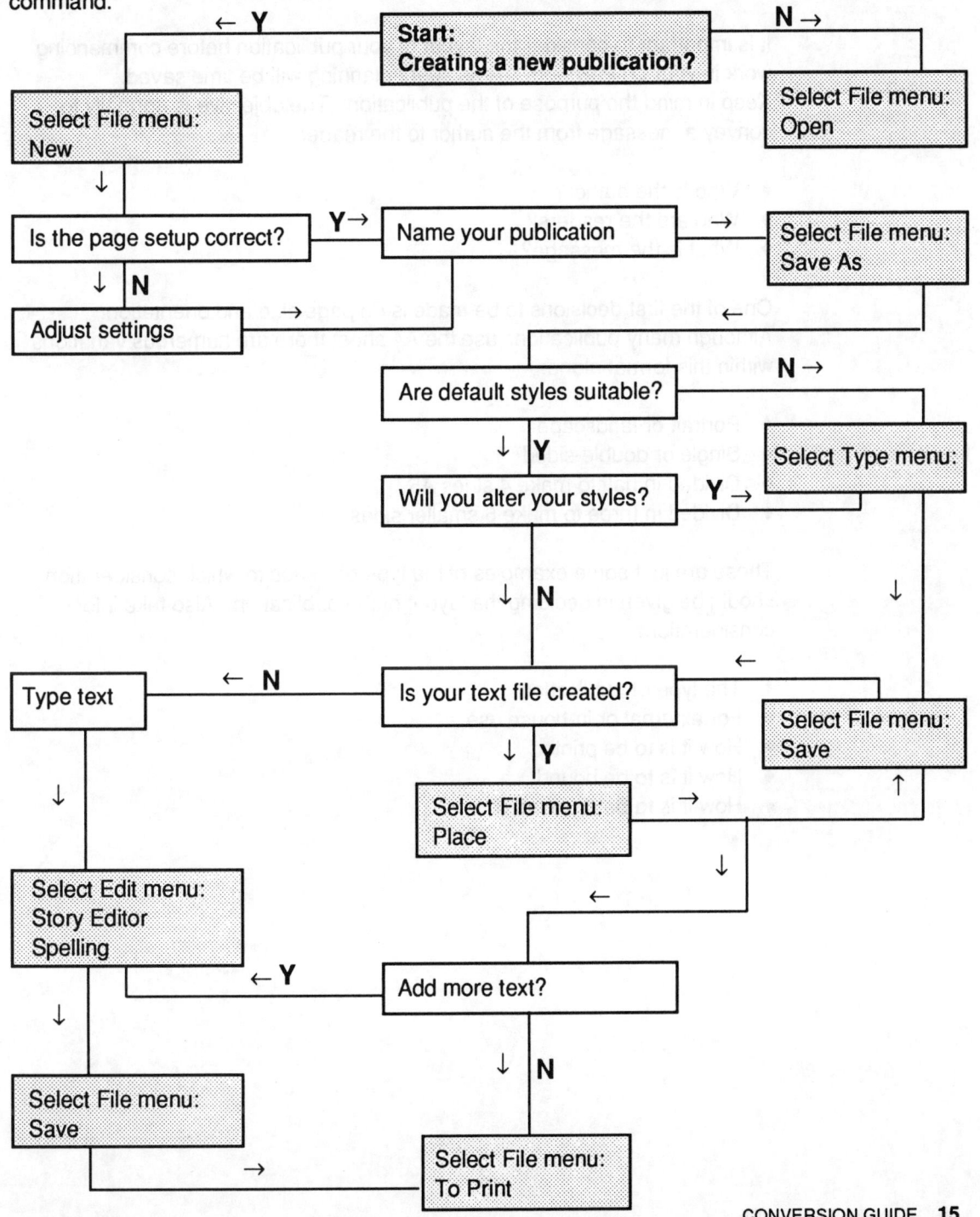

Planning the publication ▬▬▬▬▬

It is important to consider the layout of your publication before commencing work in your DTP system. Time spent planning will be time saved.
Keep in mind the purpose of the publication. The objective is normally to convey a message from the author to the reader.

♦ Who is the author?
♦ Who are the readers?
♦ What is the message?

One of the first decisions to be made is on page size and orientation. Although many publications use the A4 sheet there are numerous variations within this format alone:

♦ Portrait or landscape
♦ Single or double-sided
♦ Divided in half to make 4 sides A5
♦ Divided in three to make 6 smaller sides

These are just some examples of the type of issues to which consideration should be given in deciding the layout of the publication. Also take into consideration:

♦ The type of publication
♦ For external or in-house use
♦ How it is to be printed
♦ How it is to be bound
♦ How it is to be distributed

Production steps

1. Determine input
2. Write text using a word processor
3. Sketch or list illustration ideas
4. Determine design specifications
   - Typefaces, sizes and styles
   - Basic text format
     first line indent
     space between paragraphs
     text alignment
     headings flush left or centred
   - Basic page layout or grid
     page size
     margins
     orientation
     number of columns
   - Final page count
     may be determined by text input and pictures
5. Read text
   - Accuracy and completeness
   - Grammar and consistency
   - Design specifications
6. Edit and format text with word processor (it's easier, although PageMaker has an integral word processing package)
7. Create illustrations
   - Scanners for photographs and line drawings
   - Paint programs for fine art illustrations or line drawings
   - Drafting programs for technical illustrations
   - Spreadsheet or graph programs for graphs
8. Set up directory and copy all files to directory
9. Create master template
10. Use tools to add elements and insert text
11. Print publication
12. Copy files - backup

Part 2
Quick Reference

This Quick Reference guide sets out in concise step by step form the basic functions most frequently used by a Desktop Publishing operator. It is intended that it should act as a quick demonstration of the way to carry out every day tasks. It does assume a basic knowledge of computers and a basic knowledge of a Desktop Publishing program. It is not meant to replace a Training Guide.

The packages included in this Quick Reference are: PageMaker v4.0, Timeworks Publisher v2.0, and Ventura Publisher 3.0 GEM and Ventura Publisher v4.0 for Windows.

The following topics are covered in relation to each package:
Program basics, setting up a publication, editing a publication, printing, enhancements, character sets, sources of text and templates.

Conventions

♦ Function keys and special keys are highlighted e.g. **Ctrl O**

♦ Where one key is to be held down while a second key is pressed they will be shown highlighted together e.g. **Ctrl F5**

♦ Alternatives are indicated by *either* and *or* in italics

♦ Where <filename> or <page> occurs you are instructed to insert the name of the file or relevant page numbers

PageMaker

Introduction

Program basics
Screen layout • Screen entry area • Help • Mouse pointer
Moving around your publication • Page view • Ruler guides

Setting up a publication
Creating a document • Page layout • Master pages • Importing files
Direct text input • Paragraph styles • Indents • Tabs • Margins
Page numbering • Type specifications • Saving a document

Editing a publication
Retrieving a document • Text blocks • Editing and formatting text
Moving text • Headers and footers • Line breaks
Search and replace • Spell check • Setting up columns
Adding and deleting pages • Style sheets and templates • Kerning
Leading • Exporting files

Printing a publication
Printing • Crop marks • Thumbnails • Print to file

Enhancements
Drawing borders and lines • Drawing boxes • Shading/fill
Text rotation • Importing pictures

Sources of text
Basic concepts • PageMaker guidelines

Character sets

Introduction

PageMaker is a DTP program which is easy for the newcomer to learn. It is based on the principle of a page composition program whereby text and graphics are placed within blocks on a page.

You can type text directly into PageMaker, or you can type text using your word processor and then bring that text onto a PageMaker page. You can create simple graphics directly in PageMaker and you can bring in graphics that were created using a graphics program. Once the graphics are in PageMaker, you can easily move them around on the page, change their size and shape, duplicate them, or delete them.

PageMaker allows control of the overall layout of the publication including paper size, margins, columns, page breaks etc. It also allows control of the detailed appearance of text including the typeface, justification, type size and enhancements such as bold and italic.

To start PageMaker from Windows double click on the **Aldus** icon then double click on the **PageMaker 4.0** icon. From the opening screen click on **File New** to set up your initial document.

It is a good idea to click on the maximize button in the right hand top corner. This ensures that PM fills the screen.

Program basics ▰▰▰▰▰▰

PageMaker screen layout _____

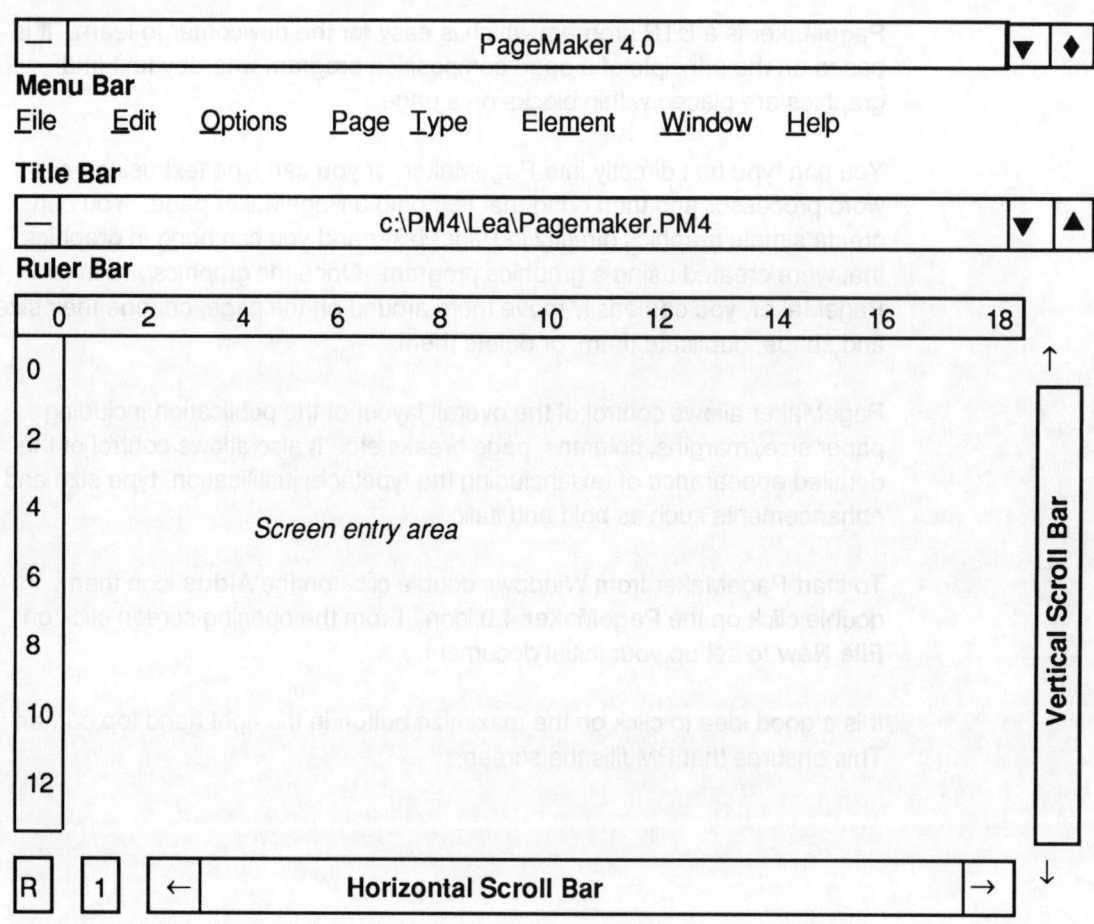

Menu Bar

File   Edit   Options   Page   Type   Element   Window   Help

Title Bar

Ruler Bar

Screen entry area

Vertical Scroll Bar

Horizontal Scroll Bar

The **Menu Bar** provides PageMaker commands
The **Title Bar** shows the document name
The **Ruler Bar** provides guides for text and graphics alignment
The **Scroll Bars** display different parts of a document
The **Page icons** indicate the master page(s) and the number of pages within the document

Screen entry area _____

Ruler

0	2	4	6	8	10	12	14	16	18	24

| 0 |
| 2 |
| 4 |
| 6 |
| 8 |
| 10 |
| 12 |
| 14 |
| 16 |

−	Tools		
↑	╲	⊢	A
▢	◯	◯	⊬

This is a text block marked

←⎯⎯ **Page** size guidelines

←⎯⎯ **Margin** guidelines

Toolbox definitions	**Speed key**
↑ **Pointer tool** to select text block and graphics	**F9**
╲ **Diagonal Line tool** to draw straight lines at any angle	**Shift F2**
⊢ **Perpendicular Line tool** to draw vertical and horizontal lines	**Shift F3**
A **Text tool** to input text into publication	**Shift F4**
⊬ **Cropping tool** to trim graphics	**Shift F8**
◯ **Circle/Oval tool** to draw ovals or circles	**Shift F7**
⬭ **Rounded Corner tool** to draw with rounded corners	**Shift F6**
▢ **Square tool** to draw squares and rectangles	**Shift F5**

Help

PageMaker Help is compatible with the standard Windows3 Help system

♦ Words with a solid underline are "Jumps" that display the Help topic they name

♦ Click the underlined topic *or* press the **Tab** key until that topic is highlighted then press **Enter** *or* press **Alt** plus the underlined letter

♦ To use Help commands and buttons at the top of the Help window press

♦ **F1** *or* select the **Help** menu

♦ **File Open** command opens any Windows Help file

♦ **File Print Topic** prints the Help topic chosen

♦ **Edit Copy** command copies the chosen Help topic to the clipboard

♦ **Edit Annotate** adds notes to Help topic

♦ **Bookmark Define** adds topic title to Bookmark menu

♦ **Index** button displays PageMaker Help menu

♦ **Back** button displays previous topic

♦ **Search** button displays a dialogue box in which to type key words to search for related Help topics

To work with Help and PageMaker windows simultaneously, resize both windows so that they do not overlap. To work with overlapping windows press **Alt Tab** to switch between windows

Mouse pointer

I-beam	text mode
Cross	line and box drawing
Pointer	Pointer tool
Crop	Cropping tool for trimming graphics

Moving around your publication

There are several ways PageMaker lets you move around in your publication:

♦ Use page icons to move from page to page

♦ Press **F12** to move to the next page

♦ Press **F11** to move to the previous page

♦ Press **Ctrl G** to use GoTo command

♦ Use **Scroll Bars** to move around the page

♦ Use **right** mouse button to move around page and change views

♦ To toggle between Fit in Window and Actual Size click **right** mouse button

♦ Press **Shift** and click **right** mouse button to go to 200% size

♦ Press and hold **Alt** key and **left** mouse button to move page on screen

♦ Use **grabber hand** to move page on screen. To use grabber hand press **Alt** and drag mouse i.e. press **left** mouse button and hold

♦ To browse through publication from page one press and hold **Shift** key and select **GoTo** page from Page menu. Click to stop

Page view

Select a page display size which best suits your work. When a document is opened PM4 will be in Fit in Window mode. The amount of page you view depends not only on your page size, but also on the size of your screen. Since a page size is normally larger than your screen size you can usually only view portions of the page.

♦ Press **Ctrl W** to access Fit in Window mode to see page set up

♦ Press **Ctrl 0** for 25% size

To select to draw rules between columns:

♦ Press **Ctrl 5** for 50% size

♦ Press **Ctrl 7** for 75% size

To select to position text and graphics:

♦ Press **Ctrl 1** to view actual size

♦ Press **Ctrl 2** to view 200% size

♦ Press **Ctrl 4** to view 400% size

Ruler guides ——————————————————————————

- ◆ Ruler guides are non-printing extensions of the tick marks on the Rulers
- ◆ They help position design elements e.g. picture frames, page numbers and borders
- ◆ Position ruler guides to help align text and graphics
- ◆ Click on *either* the horizontal *or* vertical Ruler Bar and drag a ruler guide to position
- ◆ To move a ruler guide drag it to a new position
- ◆ To delete a ruler guide drag it out of the window

Setting up a publication ▬▬▬▬▬▬

There are certain steps to follow when you first set up a publication in your DTP program. Plan your document before you start. If you have an idea of what you want and even draw a picture of your ideas, then the end result will be worth the time and effort.

This section will take you through the following procedures in setting up a publication:

♦ Creating a document
♦ Page layout and master pages
♦ Importing files and direct text input
♦ Paragraph styles
♦ Indents, tabs and margins
♦ Page numbering
♦ Type specifications

Creating a document ▬▬▬▬▬▬▬▬▬▬▬▬▬▬▬

♦ To create a document select **New** from the File menu *or* press **Ctrl N**
♦ From the Page Setup dialogue box make changes to the default settings as required
♦ Select the desired page size, orientation, start page number, number of pages, options, margins, numbering style
♦ Click on **right** marker in Title Bar to fit page to screen
♦ Click on **R** page to create master page style sheet for a single sided document
♦ To create master page layout style sheet on a double sided document click on **L** page then **R** page
♦ Click **OK** to display untitled pasteboard screen which indicates page frame and margins setup

Page layout ▬▬▬▬▬▬▬▬▬▬▬▬▬▬▬▬▬▬▬▬▬

♦ **Page Setup** in the File menu allows for all changes to a page: size, orientation, start page number, number of pages, options and margins

Master pages _____

The master page is the cornerstone in the production of a publication. It is a blueprint for every page in the publication

♦ Click **master page** icon to turn to master page
♦ Set column and ruler guides in place
♦ Create a footer
♦ Draw a box or lines as required
♦ Check set up of master page
♦ Save your publication

Importing files _____

Text files can be loaded from many different word processors as well as any ASCII text file

♦ To load a text file select **Place** from the File menu
♦ From the Place File dialogue box click on the **path** and **filename** to import
♦ The name is highlighted in the list and appears in the name field
♦ Place text as a new item, replacing entire story *or* inserting text

Several options are available when importing text

♦ *Retain format:* when checked imports the style sheet set-up; when unchecked text is placed to PageMaker's default specifications set on master page(s)
♦ *Convert quotes:* when checked PageMaker converts ordinary marks to typeset-style quotation marks
♦ *Read tags:* when checked PageMaker looks for style name tags to format paragraphs. Style name tags inserted in your word processing program should be in angle brackets and match a style defined in PageMaker e.g. <Headline>
♦ Click **OK**
♦ Pointer changes to one of the Place icons
♦ The easiest way to place a word processing file is to turn on **Autoflow** in the Options menu

Direct text input

PageMaker allows you to type text directly into your document in layout view. In addition PM4 has a built-in word processor called **Story Editor**. The benefits of Story Editor are that it is a word processor with a spelling checker, search and replace capabilities, multiple story windows and is able to display non-printing characters

♦ To enter Story Editor you must have an open publication window
♦ To open the story window at the start of a text block triple click **Pointer tool**
♦ To open story window at a layout view location click an **insertion point** in a text block with the text tool and select **Edit Story**
♦ To open a new story window select **Edit Story**
♦ Once in story view you can add a new story, type text, or import another story
♦ To leave story view click on **Edit Layout** in the Edit menu
♦ Click text I-beam in position and type
♦ New text can be entered anywhere and will form its own text block which can be moved into required position

Paragraph styles

♦ To create, edit, remove and copy paragraph styles use **Define Styles** from the Type menu
♦ A paragraph style affects the appearance of a paragraph not its content
♦ Use a paragraph style to control the font and its size, the type style (bold, italic) the alignment, tabs, indents etc.
♦ To select from the Define Styles dialogue box click on tag name
♦ Select new style, edit, remove or copy
♦ Default styles are Body text, Caption, Headline, Subhead1, and Subhead2
♦ Click **Paragraph** in the type menu to access the paragraph specifications dialogue box to set indents, paragraph space, alignment, dictionary and options

Indents

- ♦ Click on **Indents/tabs** in the Type menu to access the Indents/tabs dialogue box
- ♦ To indent first paragraph place the tip of the cursor on the lower triangle and drag it to the indent position
- ♦ To prevent the first line indent marker from moving hold down **Shift** as you point to the lower triangle
- ♦ Click **OK**

To set a *hanging indent*

- ♦ Place cursor in position
- ♦ Select **Indents/tabs**
- ♦ Click to create a tab setting
- ♦ Hold down **Shift** key, drag the bottom triangle to the right until aligned with tab and click **OK**

Tabs

- ♦ Select **Indents/tabs** from the Type menu
- ♦ Select one of four types of tabs: left, right, centre and decimal
- ♦ Click the Ruler at tab position
- ♦ To remove tab marker drag it down and out of the dialogue box
- ♦ To move tab drag it along the Ruler line

Margins

- ♦ Select **Page Setup** from the File menu to access dialogue box
- ♦ Click appropriate box to change margin settings
- ♦ Click **OK** to select changes

Page numbering

- ♦ Set automatic page number starting with page number in **Page Setup** dialogue box
- ♦ Click an insert point in place
- ♦ Press **Ctrl Shift 3** to insert page number marker on *either* master pages *or* first publication page
- ♦ To add text type on the master page followed by page number marker

Type specifications

♦ Select **Type Specifications** from the Type menu to change font, size, position, leading, case, width, track, colour and style
♦ The fonts available will depend on your printer set up

Saving a document

♦ To name and save a new publication or template click **Save As** in the File menu
♦ To save the most recent changes to your publication or template use the **Save** command from the File menu *or* press **Ctrl S**
♦ Remember to save often and make backup copies of your publication to avoid accidental loss

Editing a publication ▬▬▬▬▬▬▬▬

Retrieving a document ▬▬▬▬▬▬▬▬▬▬▬▬▬▬▬▬▬▬▬▬

- ◆ Select **Open** from the File menu to access the Open Publication dialogue box
- ◆ Scroll the Files/Directories list box to find publication
- ◆ PageMaker automatically selects the original option
- ◆ To open an untitled copy of the publication click **Copy**

Text blocks ▬▬▬▬▬▬▬▬▬▬▬▬▬▬▬▬▬▬▬▬▬▬▬▬▬▬▬▬▬

A text block defines a space on the page occupied by text. In PageMaker the text on your page is contained in text blocks. You work with text character by character but you manipulate text blocks in the same way you do graphics: as movable objects on the page. A text block can be either a single story or part of a longer story composed of a number of text blocks

- ◆ To select text use the Text tool
- ◆ To select a text block, use the Pointer tool
- ◆ The text block is bound at top and bottom by a windowshade with loops called windowshade handles
- ◆ An **empty** windowshade handle at the top of a block indicates the beginning of the story and at the end of a block tells you that the whole story has been placed
- ◆ A **plus** sign in the windowshade handle between text blocks indicates that there is text from the same story before and after that text block
- ◆ A **down** arrow in the windowshade handle indicates that there is more text to place
- ◆ Text blocks can be manipulated in many different ways: moved, deleted, cut and pasted

Editing and formatting text

The ability to format text is the cornerstone of graphic design

♦ To **edit** text click on text tool and click **mouse pointer** on text to edit

♦ To **insert** text type at cursor point

♦ To **delete** backwards press **backspace**

♦ Text must be selected to delete forwards

♦ Press **Delete** key to delete and **Shift Delete** to cut selected text

♦ Select **Font** or **Size** from the Type menu to change typeface

♦ Make selections and return to publication

Moving text

♦ Highlight text to be moved

♦ Click on **Cut** from the Edit menu

♦ Move to new location

♦ Click on **Paste** in the Edit menu and text will flow in new location

♦ A text block can be moved by holding down the **left** mouse button as you drag the text block to its new position

Headers and footers

♦ To insert headers or footers in PageMaker set the text up on the master page

♦ Move to **Master page**

♦ Type text in position

♦ Move text block as required on master page(s)

♦ Click on another page to view

Line breaks

♦ Press **Shift Enter** to create a new line within the existing paragraph
♦ This feature is an advantage when setting tabs in that you can format a whole section rather than each paragraph
♦ Remember a paragraph is a section of text which ends when you press **Enter**

Search and replace

PageMaker allows for a search and replace facility within its built-in word processor - Story Editor
♦ Select text block
♦ Select **Story Editor** from the Edit menu
♦ To search only select **Find** from the Edit menu to access dialogue box
♦ To search and replace select **Change** from the Edit menu to access dialogue box
♦ Complete search information
♦ Select options: match case or whole word if required
♦ Select search criteria: selected text, current story, all stories
♦ Click **Find**

Spell check

PageMaker's word processing facility - Story Editor - allows you to check your publication for misspelled and mistyped words
♦ Select text
♦ Select **Story Editor** from the Edit menu
♦ Select **Spelling** from the Edit menu to access dialogue box from which you can check for spelling mistakes
♦ Select search criteria: selected text, current story, all stories
♦ When an unknown word is displayed select: ignore, replace or add

Setting up columns _____

- Every page has at least a single column which is the area between the margins
- Select **Column Guides** from the Options menu to display the dialogue box
- Select number of columns
- Change space between columns if necessary
- Click **OK**
- If all or most of the pages in your publication have the same number of columns create the column guides on the master page

Adding and deleting pages _____

To add pages
- Select **Insert Pages** from the Page menu to access dialogue box
- Complete no. of pages, before, after or between current pages information and click **OK**

To delete pages
- Select **Remove Pages** from the Page menu to access dialogue box
- Complete page numbers
- Click **OK**

Style sheets and templates _____

Style sheets
A style sheet is a collection of styles or formatting information that you apply to a publications paragraphs to define their appearance. The information includes such specifications as typeface and type size, line spacing and paragraph spacing.
- PageMaker includes default styles for No Style, Body Text, Caption, Headline, Subhead 1 and Subhead 2

To define new styles
- Select **Define Styles** from the Type menu to access the dialogue box
- Click on **New** and select No style in the based on box
- Click and complete the buttons: type, paragraph, tabs

To copy an existing style sheet from another publication
- Select **Define Styles** from the Type menu
- Click **copy** and in the Copy Styles dialogue box double click the publication from which styles are to be copied

To apply individual styles

♦ Use Text tool *either* to select text *or* to click an insertion point in paragraph
♦ To ensure Style Palette box is visible click **Style Palette** from the Windows menu to display the box
♦ Click on style choice in palette

PageMaker templates

PageMaker provides 25 templates and 10 grids which can be used to create your own publications or can be used just as they are.

Template files contain dummy text and graphics placeholders; replace the placeholders with your own text and graphics to end up with a specialised document.

PageMaker templates, if loaded onto your computer, are in a sub-directory called 'templates'. Constant items throughout a template, e.g. column guides and page-number characters, are placed on the master pages.

Style sheets have been attached to each template to control how text looks on the page. To format new text apply the appropriate style from the style palette. To change text formatting make changes to the style sheet itself.

The templates are set up to print on a standard PostScript-language printer. If your printer is different then you will need to change PageMaker's printer settings.

To open a template file from PageMaker

♦ Select **Open** from the File menu
♦ Double click on the template **filename** in the Open Publication dialogue box

The templates included with PageMaker are:
Application, Avery labels, Brochure 1, Brochure 2, Business cards, Calendar, Catalogue, Directory, Envelope, Financial sheet, Invoice, Letterhead, Manual1, Manual2, Manual3, Memo, Newsletter1, Newsletter2, Newsletter3, Price list, Proposal and Purchase Order
Keep in mind that there is also a character set template and the use of this is defined on page 51.

Kerning

Kerning adjusts the space between individual text characters. Track kerning in Pagemaker can be applied automatically to provide a wide range of options

To track kern

♦ Select text

♦ Select **Track** from the Type menu to access the list of options: no track, very loose, loose, normal, tight, very tight

♦ With **Pair** kerning checked in the Spacing Attributes box, PageMaker automatically kerns character pairs specified by font designer

To kern manually

♦ Place insertion point between two characters

♦ Press **Ctrl +** (on numeric keypad) to increase space

♦ Press **Ctrl -** (on numeric keypad) to decrease space

Leading

Leading refers to the vertical distance between individual lines of text. As a general rule the leading should be at least 20% greater than the font size e.g.12 point leading for 10 point type

♦ Select **Leading** from Type menu and adjust as necessary

Please note that double spaced lines on 10 point text would mean leading set at 24 point

Exporting files

♦ Select text

♦ Select **Export** from the File menu to save text from your publication for use outside PageMaker

♦ Select path, enter <filename>, complete export details, entire story or selected text only and options if required

♦ Select file format

♦ Click **OK**

Printing a publication

Printing

The hard copy of any publication is the end result of your hard work. It is also a means of viewing the proofs of your publication so that adjustments and amendments can be made before the production is complete.

♦ Click on **Print** in the File menu *or* press **Ctrl P** to display the Print dialogue box

♦ Complete sections as required: copies, collage, reverse order, page range, scaling, even/odd pages, duplex and options

♦ Click **OK** to print

Crop marks

♦ To insert crop marks to indicate the page boundaries click on **Crop Marks** in the options section of the Print dialogue box

Thumbnails

PageMaker has the ability to print up to 64 thumbnails (miniature copy of a page) on a page to allow you to preview your publication

♦ Select **Thumbnails** from the options section of the Print dialogue box

Print to file

This is useful when taking your publication to a service bureau for printing on a high resolution imagesetter

♦ Select **Print** from the File menu

♦ Select **Setup**

♦ Select **Options**

♦ Select **Header**

♦ Send Header to File

Enhancements ■■■■■■■■■■■■

The benefits of a desktop publishing package over a word processing program can be seen in the ease with which graphics, boxes and tables can be added to your text. This section covers:

♦ Drawing borders and lines
♦ Drawing boxes
♦ Special effects: shading/filling
♦ Text rotation
♦ Importing pictures

Drawing borders and lines _____

♦ Select Graphics tool from the toolbox
♦ Select the Straight Line tool to draw a straight line
♦ Place horizontal and vertical ruler guides in position
♦ Click icon on first ruler guide intersection
♦ Hold **left** mouse button down and drag pointer to second ruler guide intersection
♦ Release mouse button
♦ To view line position click on **Guides** in Options menu to temporarily remove guide lines
♦ Click **Guides** again to replace guide lines
♦ To adjust line style and thickness select line and click on **Line** in the
♦ Element menu
♦ Make selection
♦ Return to publication

Drawing boxes _____

- ◆ Select Graphic tool from toolbox
- ◆ Select Rectangle or Rounded Corner tool
- ◆ Place horizontal and vertical ruler lines
- ◆ Click icon on first ruler guide intersection
- ◆ Click and hold mouse button down and drag to size using ruler guidelines for position
- ◆ Select box to adjust box lines style and thickness
- ◆ Select **Line** from the Element menu
- ◆ Make selection
- ◆ Return to publication

Shading/fill _____

- ◆ Select shape
- ◆ Select **Fill** from the Element menu to access fill selection
- ◆ Make selection
- ◆ To select shapes or text hidden behind a filled shape press and hold **Ctrl** while clicking the filled shape with the pointer tool

Text rotation _____

- ◆ Text can be rotated in 90-degree increments in PageMaker
- ◆ Text must be in a single text block
- ◆ Use Pointer tool to select text
- ◆ Select **Text Rotation** from the Element menu to access the dialogue box which displays four 'A' icons
- ◆ Make selection
- ◆ Click **OK**
- ◆ To edit text block go to Story View by triple clicking in text block with pointer tool

Importing pictures

- Select **Place** from the File menu to access Place File dialogue box
- Select file from Files/Directories list
- Complete Place information:
  If nothing is selected: as independent graphic to add selected graphic to your publication
  If graphic is selected: replace selected independent graphic
  If an insertion point is placed: as inline graphic to add a graphic to publication at the insertion point

You can import four types of graphics created with other programs:

- Paint-type or bitmapped graphics
- Draw-type or object oriented graphics (such as Windows metafile)
- EPS - encapsulated postscript graphics
- Scanned graphics saved in TIFF format

Cropping the picture

- Select Cropping tool from toolbox
- Select picture
- Position Cropping tool so that graphic handle shows through the centre of the tool
- Hold down left mouse button
- When Cropping tool becomes a double headed arrow drag until the part of the picture you want is displayed

Sizing graphics

- To size a graphic drag one of its handles
- Click on graphic
- Point at one of the selection handles
- Drag to resize
- Release button and graphics box changes size

Scaling graphics

- Hold down **Shift** and drag a corner handle
- To magic stretch (resize proportionally and match printer resolution) hold down **Shift and Ctrl** while dragging

Sources of text ▬▬▬▬▬▬

Even though text can be typed directly in your DTP package, it is not the most efficient means of text input. Using a word processor means that the input process is not restricted to one person (the DTP operator) and also that preliminary drafts may be perfected prior to the text being imported into your publication.

PageMaker has included a search and replace facility and spell check in version 4. Word processing programs however, still have a major advantage; the ability to correct errors quickly and efficiently. This is one of the reasons why it is advisable to prepare your document in your word processing package, and not directly in your DTP publication.

In PageMaker the word processing programs accepted will depend upon the filters set up at installation. An assumption has been made that all filters available for your program have been installed.

The DTP publication on page 49 has been produced from a word processing package. The example of this setup is laid out with paragraph and tab format characters revealed.

Basic concepts ▬▬▬▬▬▬▬▬▬▬▬▬▬▬▬▬▬▬▬▬▬▬▬▬▬

There are certain formats which are common to all DTP packages and these are explained below.

♦ Paragraph formatting should be left justified and single spaced
♦ Unless a double space is required between paragraphs press **Enter** only once
♦ Alter tab positions in your word processor only if you want a neat draft print out. Ensure that you press **Tab** only once between tabbed columns
♦ Use the Tab key not the indent key. Your paragraph styles are set in your DTP program

The following section outlines the handling of tags and embedded codes.

PageMaker guidelines _____

PageMaker can import text from word processing, spreadsheet and database programs as well as from other PageMaker publications. This section however, will cover preparing a document in your word processing package for importing in to PageMaker.

In PageMaker to import successfully you must have the filters installed (this is assumed) and name the file with an extension Pagemaker recognises. PageMaker files created on a Macintosh can also be imported into PageMaker on an IBM compatible machine (see your manual for further information on how to do this).

The example on page 49 shows a document prepared in a word processing program with formatting codes revealed.

Tagging text with a paragraph style

Unless tagged a text file imported in to PageMaker will have [No Style] selected. Therefore it is advisable to set up paragraph tags in your word processor (even if you only set up body text)

♦ To tag a paragraph type a style name enclosed within angle brackets at the beginning of a paragraph e.g. <Body text>
♦ Paragraph style applies until a new tag name is entered in angle brackets
♦ If a style-name does not match an existing PageMaker style PageMaker creates a new style based on the formatting applied to the style-name tag in the wordprocessing program

Embedded codes

These are not necessary as PageMaker imports styles applied to text in your word processing program. That is, PageMaker imports whatever formatting information was specified.

For example if you use your word processor to embolden text PageMaker will import it as bold. The same applies if you change your text to italics or underlined text. These formatting attributes set up in your word processor are imported in to PageMaker.

Word processing packages

PageMaker supports most word processing packages. These are listed below with the filename extensions that PageMaker recognises for each:

ASCII (text-only files)	.TXT
DCA file format	.DCA, .RFT
DEC WPS Plus	.DX
DisplayWrite	.DCA, .RFT
Rich Text Format	.RTF
WordPerfect 5.0, 5.1	.WP5
WordPerfect 4.2	.WP
Word 3.0 - 5.5	.DOC
Word for Windows	.DOC
Windows Write	.WRI
WordStar 3.3-6.0	.WS
MultiMate/Advantage IV	.DOC
Olitext Plus	.OTX
PC Write	.PCW
Samna Ami Professional	.SAM
Samna Word	.SAM
XyWrite III Plus 3.53	.XY3
Wang	.IWP,.DOX

Notes

WordPerfect 5 & 5.1

♦ When you hold down the **Shift** key as you place or import files PageMaker displays the WordPerfect 5.0-5.1 import filters so that you can determine whether and how the styles will be imported into the Styles palette

Word for Windows

♦ When you hold down the **Shift** key as you place or import files PageMaker opens the Word for Windows import filter dialogue box

Word 3.0-5.5

♦ PageMaker imports Word styles and formatting

ASCII text files

♦ When you import a text only file with no style-name tags PageMaker applies its own publication defaults for type, paragraph formats, tabs etc When you place a text-only file PageMaker displays the Smart ASCII import filter dialogue box which helps address two problems of importing text-only files:

   ♦ extra carriage returns
   ♦ spaces used to align columns of a table or to indent paragraphs

Document set up in word processing for importing to PageMaker

<Headline>A DTP Feature ¶

¶

<Subhead>Importing Text¶

¶

<Body text>Text prepared by several operators can easily and readily be read in to your Desktop Publishing package, be it **PageMaker**, **Ventura Publisher** *or* **Timeworks Publisher**.¶

By this means your DTP operator can receive work prepared in several different sources. Of course the criteria needs to be set prior to the WP operator starting the document. It also depends on the package as to how the details should be set up. This article illustrates basic set up only and gives examples of a few of the extensive tagging and embedded codes you can use.¶

¶

¶

©Lea Weston

Publication produced from word processed document

A DTP Feature

Importing Text

Text prepared by several operators can easily and readily be read in to your Desktop Publishing package, be it **PageMaker**, **Ventura Publisher** *or* **Timeworks Publisher**.

By this means your DTP operator can receive work prepared in several different sources. Of course the criteria needs to be set prior to the WP operator starting the document. It also depends on the package as to how the details should be set up. This article illustrates basic set up only and gives examples of a few of the extensive tagging and embedded codes you can use.

©Lea Weston

Character sets ▬▬▬▬▬▬▬▬▬▬▬▬▬

Every character that you see on your screen is represented internally by a number, called its *ASCII code*. If you have graphics capability and your printer is capable of printing that character you can produce foreign-language and scientific text readily and easily.

All computer packages with the correct printer capabilities are able to print from the ASCII list. To access these additional characters you hold down the **Alt** key and type the number using the numeric keypad. (Note that it will not work if you use the numbers along the top of the keyboard.) The diacritical marks (umlauts, tildes, etc) used in languages other than English can be inserted into an English document. For example to get the French é hold down **Alt** and press **130** on the numeric keypad. Release the **Alt** key and the é appears on the screen.

Under the Windows environment additional characters and symbols are available in the same manner. To insert these characters you type in a four digit number, rather than the three for ASCII. The method remains the same, i.e. press **Alt 0233** for the French é.

PageMaker has made it easy for you to find out what characters are available with what ASCII codes by supplying a template called CHARSET.PT4 which is found in the \PM4\TEMPLATES directory.

♦ To use this template open a copy of **CHARSET.PM4**
♦ Ensure your target printer is selected
♦ With the Text tool click in story and press **Ctrl A** to highlight the entire story
♦ From the Type menu select the required font and either view the screen display or print the page

The chart on the following page indicates the standard ASCII character sets for one typeface only. Remember that you may have a number of fonts, including Symbols and Dingbats which will give you different results.

Aldus character set

33	!	72	H	111	o	150	û	0189	•	0228	ä
34	"	73	I	112	p	151	ù	0190	•	0229	å
35	#	74	J	113	q	152	ÿ	0191	¿	0230	æ
36	$	75	K	114	r	153	Ö	0192	À	0231	ç
37	%	76	L	115	s	154	Ü	0193	Á	0232	è
38	&	77	M	116	t	155	¢	0194	Â	0233	é
39	'	78	N	117	u	156	£	0195	Ã	0234	ê
40	(	79	O	118	v	157	¥	0196	Ä	0235	ë
41	)	80	P	119	w	158	p	0197	Å	0236	ì
42	*	81	Q	120	x	159	f	0198	Æ	0237	í
43	+	82	R	121	y	160	á	0199	Ç	0238	î
44	,	83	S	122	z	161	í	0200	È	0239	ï
45	-	84	T	123	{	162	ó	0201	É	0240	•
46	.	85	U	124	|	163	ú	0202	Ê	0241	ñ
47	/	86	V	125	}	164	ñ	0203	Ë	0242	ò
48	0	87	W	126	~	165	Ñ	0204	Ì	0243	ó
49	1	88	X	127	•	166	ª	0205	Í	0244	ô
50	2	89	Y	128	Ç	167	º	0206	Î	0245	õ
51	3	90	Z	129	ü	168	¿	0207	Ï	0246	ö
52	4	91	[	130	é	0169	©	0208	•	0247	•
53	5	92	\	131	â	0170	ª	0209	Ñ	0248	ø
54	6	93	]	132	ä	0171	«	0210	Ò	0249	ù
55	7	94	^	133	à	0172	¬	0211	Ó	0250	ú
56	8	95	_	134	å	0173	-	0212	Ô	0251	û
57	9	96	'	135	ç	0174	®	0213	Õ	0252	ü
58	:	97	a	136	ê	0175	‾	0214	Ö	0253	•
59	;	98	b	137	ë	0176	°	0215	•	0254	•
60	<	99	c	138	è	0177	•	0216	Ø	**C=Ctrl**	
61	=	100	d	139	ï	0178	•	0217	Ù	**S=Shift**	
62	>	101	e	140	î	0179	•	0218	Ú	CS=	—
63	?	102	f	141	ì	0180	´	0219	Û	C=	–
64	@	103	g	142	Ä	0181	•	0220	Ü	CS[	"
65	A	104	h	143	Å	0182	¶	0221	•	CS]	"
66	B	105	i	144	É	0183	·	0222	•	C[	'
67	C	106	j	145	æ	0184	¸	0223	ß	C]	'
68	D	107	k	146	Æ	0185	•	0224	à	CS8	•
69	E	108	l	147	ô	0186	º	0225	á	CS7	¶
70	F	109	m	148	ö	0187	»	0226	â	CS6	§
71	G	110	n	149	ò	0188	•	0227	ã	CSG	®
										CSO	©

These characters are available in PageMaker. Press and hold the **Alt** key and press the number from the number keypad. When the **Alt** key is released the character will appear.

Timeworks Publisher

Introduction

Program basics
Screen layout • Item selector dialogue box • Toolbox definitions
Graphics icons • Help • Mouse pointer
Moving around your publication • Page view

Setting up a publication
Creating a document • Page layout • Master pages • Direct text input
Importing files • Paragraph styles • Indents • Tabs • Margins
Page numbering • Type specifications • Saving a document

Editing a publication
Retrieving a document • Text blocks • Editing and formatting text
Moving text • Headers and footers • Line breaks • Search and replace
Spell check • Setting up columns • Adding and deleting pages
Style sheets • Kerning • Leading • Exporting files

Printing a publication
Printing • Crop marks

Enhancements
Drawing borders and lines • Drawing boxes • Shading/filling
Text rotation • Importing pictures

Sources of text

Character sets

Introduction ▬▬▬▬▬▬▬▬▬▬▬▬▬▬▬▬

Timeworks Publisher is a frame-based Desktop Publishing program which is as happy running on slower processors as it is in a high powered environment. It is a budget priced package which can be run on an 8086-based machine or 286 and faster processors. It runs under the GEM environment and comes supplied with GEM version 3.11 and now supports both expanded and extended memory allowing the creation of documents with up to 999 pages.

Because Timeworks is a frame-based DTP program it means that everything laid on to the page has to be typed, drawn or imported into a pre-defined frame. Unlike other DTP programs though, you don't have to define different types of frames for text and graphics objects. Both text and graphics can be placed in frames which can be linked and text can flow from one frame to another. Also, new frames can be created as you need them.

Timeworks has adopted the paragraph style which enables layout and typography to be modified en bloc. This facility comes in to its own when creating longer documents. The seven fonts supplied with Timeworks Publisher are Typografica fonts, and you can have fonts in virtually any size and style you want but only one width for each point size.

A Windows Bridge has been supplied with the product, consisting of a PIF file and icon, which allows it to be run from the Windows desktop - but in full screen mode, not in a window.

To start Timeworks from GEM make sure you are in the GEM directory and type **GEM** to display the GEM desktop. Double click on the **Publish** folder icon and then double click on the **Publish.App** icon. The other alternative is to ensure you are in the directory where Timeworks Publisher is installed and type **Publish**. When you load Timeworks Publisher you are in Frame mode and the mouse pointer looks like an open cross.

Program basics

Timeworks Publisher screen layout

Menu Bar

File   Edit   Options   Page   Style   Text   Graphics   Help   Publish

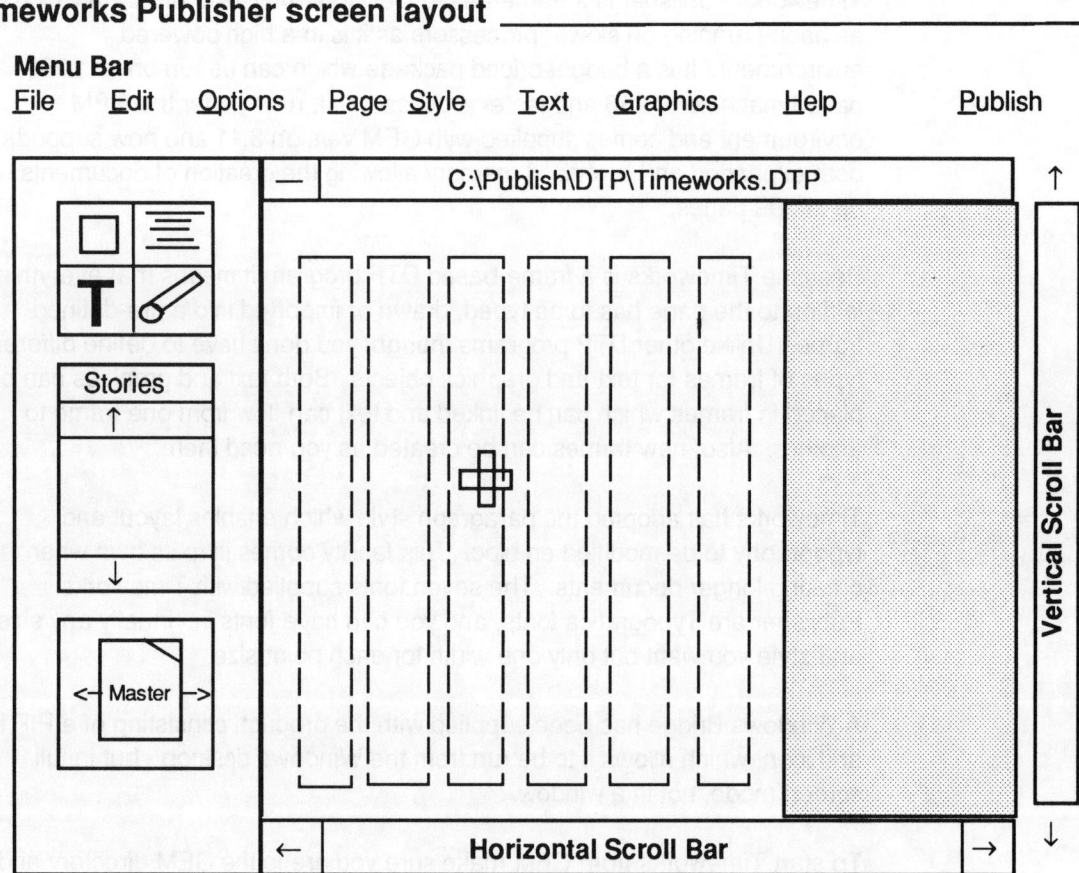

The **Menu Bar** provides Timeworks commands
The **Scroll Bars** display different parts of a document
The **Page Icons** indicate the master page
The **Column Guides** display the guidelines for drawing frames
The **Toolbox** contains frame mode, paragraph mode, text mode and graphics mode
The **Title Bar** shows the path and document name
The **Browser** in frame mode contains text or picture file names, in paragraph mode contains paragraph styles, in text mode contains text styles list and in graphics contains graphic drawing tools icons

Item selector dialogue box

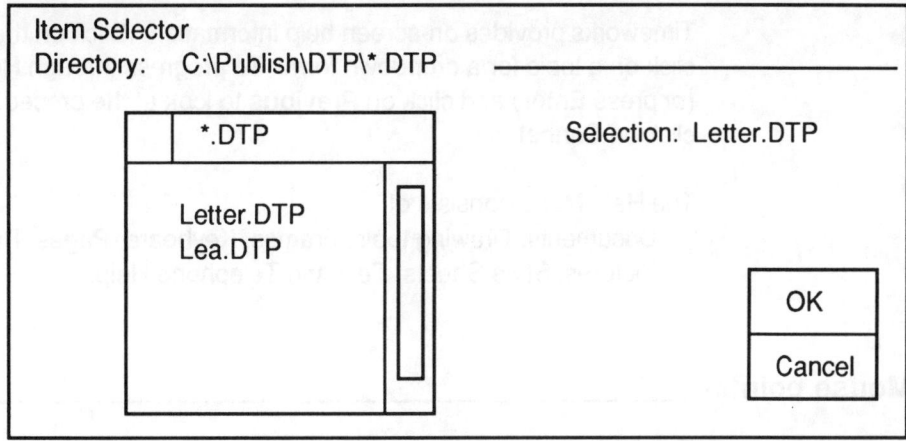

Toolbox definitions

Frame mode to draw, resize and move frames as well as import text

Paragraph mode to work with entire paragraphs of text using paragraph styles

Text mode to type, edit and restyle text

Graphics mode to draw simple graphics such as lines, circles and rectangles

Graphics icons

Straight line icon

Rectangle icon

Polyline icon

Rounded corners icon

Circle icon

Oval icon

Help _____

Timeworks provides on-screen help information. Click on the Help menu and click on a topic for a dropdown form. To progress through Help click on **Next** (*or* press **Enter**) and click on **Previous** to look at the preceding page. To exit click on **Cancel**.

The Help Menu consists of:
Documents, Drawing tools, Frames, Keyboard, Pages, Paragraph styles, Pictures, Style Sheets, Text and Telephone Help.

Mouse pointer _____

Pointer	outside work area
Open cross	frame mode
¶	paragraph mode
I-beam	text mode
Crosshair	graphics mode

Moving around your publication _____

♦ Click on arrows on page icon to move from page to page, *or*
♦ Click on **GoTo Page** in the Page menu
♦ Press **Ctrl PgUp** to display first page
♦ Press **Ctrl PgDn** to display last page

Page view _____

♦ Press **Alt 0** for half size
♦ Press **Alt 1** for 3/4 size
♦ Press **Alt 2** for actual size for text editing
♦ Press **Alt 3** for double size for detailed work
♦ Press **Alt 4** for full page
♦ Press **Alt 5** for two pages view

Setting up a publication ▬▬▬▬▬▬▬▬▬▬

There are certain steps to follow when you first set up a publication in your Desktop Publishing program. The most important point to remember is to plan your document before you start. If you have an idea of what you want and even draw a picture of your ideas then the end result will be worth the time and effort.

This section will take you through the following procedures in setting up a publication:

♦ Creating a document
♦ Page layout and master pages
♦ Importing files and direct text input
♦ Paragraph styles
♦ Indents, tabs and margins
♦ Page numbering
♦ Type specifications
♦ Saving a document

Creating a document ───────────────────────

♦ To create a new document click on **New** in the File menu
♦ To load a style sheet click on **Yes** but to create a new style sheet click on **No**

You must set up your page format from the displayed menu

♦ Select paper size, orientation etc to change default settings
♦ After setting up the page format click on **OK**

With Timeworks the first step is to draw the frames which will hold your text and graphics. To ensure all pages in your document are set with the same layout draw your frames on the master page

♦ To display the master page click on **GoTo Page** in the Page menu

The master page has six column guides to help you draw the frames and position them

♦ Place the mouse pointer at the top left hand corner of the first column guide. Drag the mouse pointer to the right and down to create a frame the size you want
♦ To change a frame size click in the frame then position the mouse pointer on one of the handles and drag the frame by the handle

Page layout _____

♦ You must set up your page format before anything else as you cannot change it later
♦ When you click **No** to a style sheet in a new document **Page Format** dialogue box allows you to select paper size, orientation and master pages set up
♦ After setting up your page format click **OK**

Master pages _____

♦ To look really professional use the same basic layout on every page
♦ The Master Page acts as a template for any new pages
   Click on **GoTo Page** in the Page menu and click **GoTo Master Page**
♦ Add header or footer
♦ Specify basic column layout
♦ Define left and right, top and bottom margins
♦ Add graphics or enhancements as required
♦ Save your style sheet

Direct text input _____

♦ To enter text directly in a frame click on the **Text** icon and position the cursor where text is to be placed and type
♦ Text will automatically be placed in the default body text style

Importing files _____

One way of placing files in a document is to import a text file created in another program such as your word processor. Unless otherwise noted all imported text is styled as body text. It is possible however to pre-tag text before importing

To tag a paragraph with a style
♦ Type the style name at the beginning of the first line enclosed in angle brackets e.g. <Headline>

To load a file prepared in a word processing program
♦ Click on **Import Text** in the File menu
♦ Click on the text format name and then click on **OK** to display the item selector to select the story to import

Text files imported: Microsoft Word 5, WordPerfect 5, DCA/RFT format for Displaywrite 3 and above, Locoscript, Lotus Manuscript, MultiMate, Office Writer, Samna Word, Volkswriter 3 and WordStar 2000 as well as ASCII text files

♦ Click on the text name and then click on **OK**
♦ The imported text is placed in the browser and is ready to be placed in the document
♦ Go to the page where text is to be placed
♦ To place text in a frame select the frame then click on the text name in the browser
♦ If part of the story is unplaced the frame will have a dotted bottom edge
♦ To place the rest of the text select another frame and then click on name in browser
♦ To import a long story select **Autoflow Text** in the Text menu
♦ The imported story should retain all text styles set up in your word processor

Paragraph styles

Every paragraph in a Timeworks Publisher document is tagged with a single paragraph style which controls the appearance of text e.g. typeface, point size, hyphenation, justification and text style

♦ Click on the **Paragraph** icon to switch to paragraph mode

The cursor changes to a paragraph symbol in the work area

When Paragraph mode is selected the current paragraph styles are listed in the browser

To *change a paragraph style*

♦ Click the mouse pointer on **Paragraph**
♦ Then click on style name in the browser

To *create a new paragraph style*

♦ Double click on the name of an existing style which is close to the style to create
♦ Click on **new style** in the Paragraph style form
♦ Press **ESC** to delete the old name and type in the new style name
♦ Set up features from the paragraph style form and click on **OK**
♦ To change a paragraph style double click on the name in the browser then click on **Paragraph Style** in the Text menu

Indents

♦ Click on **Paragraph Style** in the Text menu and then set margins and indents from **Dimensions** dialogue box

♦ To set the amount of space above a paragraph use **Space Above** setting

♦ To set a hanging indent set a first line left indent smaller than the left indent then click **OK**

♦ Hanging indents are particularly useful for numbering paragraph indents

Tabs

♦ Click on **Paragraph Style** in the Text menu

♦ Click on **Set Tabs**

♦ If paragraph style is not Table select **Table Justification**

♦ Select number of tabs to set

♦ Click on position *or* width in **List Tabs** by box

♦ Enter tab position

♦ Select tab type (left, right, centre *or* decimal)

♦ Choose leader type (spaces, dots, underscore)

♦ Set up leader spacing if required

♦ To duplicate tabs click on **Copy Selected** tab to all others

♦ Click on **OK** to complete

Margins

♦ Margins are pre-defined by the frames

♦ Refer to indents for adjustments to margins within a frame

Page numbering _____

- To insert a page number you must set up either a header or footer
- Select **Headers and footers** from the Text menu to display dialogue box
- Click on Header or Footer
- Select left, right *or* all
- Type **#** to insert current page number and **%** to insert last page number e.g. Type **Page # of %** to give *Page 1 of 15*
- To start page numbering from other than page 1 type the preferred number in **Start Numbering From** page box
- Specify distance from top or bottom of page
- Click **OK** to create

Type specifications _____

- Select **Style** menu to change font and size and attributes such as bold, italic etc
- The fonts available are those set up when you installed Timeworks and will depend on your printer set up

Saving a document _____

- Timeworks default new document name is **Untitled.DTP**
- Click on **Save As** in the File menu
- When Item selector box appears click on **DTP** folder to open it
- Type <filename> and extension e.g. **LEA.DTP**
- Click on **OK**

Editing a publication ▰▰▰▰▰▰▰▰▰▰▰▰

No matter how well you plan your publication before you start, inevitably there are changes to be made before the document is complete. This section covers:

♦ Retrieving a document
♦ Text blocks
♦ Editing, formatting and moving text
♦ Headers and footers
♦ Line breaks
♦ Search and replace
♦ Spell check
♦ Setting up columns
♦ Adding and deleting pages
♦ Stylesheets
♦ Kerning and leading
♦ Exporting files

Retrieving a document _____

♦ To open a document click **Open** in the File menu
♦ When Item Selector appears select the document name to load and click **OK**

Text blocks _____

♦ A text block can be moved, deleted, copied or restyled
♦ To mark a block of text in text mode highlight the area using the mouse
♦ pointer *or* the **shift click** method
♦ Click at the start of the block of text and **shift click** at the end of the block to highlight text in reverse video

Note: To shift click hold the **Shift** key down and click the mouse at the same time

Editing and formatting text _____

- ◆ Click on **Text mode** and click mouse pointer on text to edit
- ◆ Press **backspace** to delete backwards and **delete** key to delete to the right of the cursor
- ◆ To change typeface select Style menu and click on **Font/Size**
- ◆ Make selections and click **OK**
- ◆ To change text style click on selection in browser *or* from Style menu

Moving text _____

- ◆ Highlight text to be moved
- ◆ Click on **Cut** from the Edit menu
- ◆ Move to new location
- ◆ Click on **Paste** from Edit menu and text will flow in new location

Headers and footers _____

- ◆ Select **Headers and footers** from the Text menu to display dialogue box
- ◆ Click on Header or Footer
- ◆ Select left, right or all
- ◆ Specify distance from top or bottom of page
- ◆ Click **OK** to create

Line breaks _____

- ◆ Press **Ctrl Enter** at text cursor position to move text to the right of the cursor on to the next line without starting a new paragraph

Search and replace

- Only works from the position of the text cursor to document end
- Click on **Search and Replace** from the Text menu
- Enter text string to replace
- Enter replacement text
- Select upper/lower case details - ignore or match
- Select substitution details - one, some or all
- Click **OK**

Spell check

Not available

Setting up columns

- Column guides are boxes with dotted outlines which are not printed out
- Click on **Set Column Guides** in Options menu to change number of column guides
- Click on arrows to increase or decrease the number of columns
- Up to 9 column guides permitted per page
- Make any changes to margins or gutter space from this dialogue box
  Click **OK**

Adding and deleting pages

- Add or delete pages from the Page menu
- Maximum number of pages in one document is 999
- To add pages complete dialogue box for number of pages, before or after current page and click **OK**
- To delete pages complete dialogue box with first page to delete and number of pages and click **OK**

Style sheets

The style sheet is a file which contains the page format chosen, the master page set up and paragraph styles designed

♦ Click on **Save Style Sheet** in the File menu to save the document format
♦ To retrieve a style sheet click on **New** in the File menu. Remember to click on **Yes** when asked to load a style sheet
♦ Select **Style Sheet** from the Item Selector

Kerning

Kerning is a printers term for adjusting the spacing between letters on a line. Because of their shape some letters can look unbalanced when evenly spaced apart

♦ To move letters closer together place the text cursor between the letters and press **Alt K**
♦ Each use of **Alt K** reduces the space by half a point
♦ Alternative method is to click on **Kern** in the Text menu and enter the amount of extra kerning in the points box
♦ Click **OK** to apply kerning

Leading

♦ Leading is the spacing between lines of text
♦ Leading should be proportional to the point size of the text and the size of the lower case letters
♦ A good guideline is leading 20% greater than the point size e.g. 12 point leading for 10 point text
♦ Therefore double spaced lines would be 24 point for 10 point text
♦ Click on **Leading** in the paragraph dimensions form to set leading

Exporting files _____

♦ Text to be exported to a word processor must be saved in ASCII format
♦ Click on the story in the browser
♦ Click **Export Text** in the File menu to display the Item Selector box
♦ Select path and folder in which to save the file
♦ File extension will be .ASC
♦ Click **OK** to export the story

Printing a publication ██████████████

The hard copy of any publication is the end result of your hard work. If in doubt as to how it will look from the screen image then produce a printed copy and view the document layout. Amendments and adjustments can then be made.

Printing

♦ Click on **Print** in the File menu to display the Print dialogue box which allows you to select number of copies, page range, forward or reverse order etc
♦ Press **backspace** to edit range of pages and number of copies
♦ Maximum number of copies you can print is 99
♦ Maximum number of pages is 999
♦ Click **OK**
♦ Press **Esc** to stop printing before completion

Crop marks

Not available

Enhancements ▬▬▬▬▬

The benefits of a Desktop Publishing package over a word processing program can be seen in the ease with which graphics, boxes and tables can be added to your text. This section covers:
- ◆ Drawing borders and lines
- ◆ Drawing boxes
- ◆ Special effects: shading/filling
- ◆ Text rotation
- ◆ Importing pictures

Drawing borders and lines ▬▬▬▬▬▬▬▬▬▬▬▬▬▬▬▬▬▬

- ◆ Click on **Graphics** tool then click in frame to select
- ◆ Select drawing tool
- ◆ Select the straight line icon to draw a line
- ◆ Click and hold mouse button down
- ◆ Drag to end of line point
- ◆ The line is surrounded by a graphics frame with handles
- ◆ To adjust line style and thickness click on **Line Style** in the Graphics menu

Drawing boxes ▬▬▬▬▬▬▬▬▬▬▬▬▬▬▬▬▬▬▬▬▬▬▬▬▬

- ◆ Click on **Graphics** tool then select frame
- ◆ Click on **Rectangle drawing tool** to draw a box
- ◆ Click and hold mouse button down and drag to size and position of box
- ◆ The box is surrounded by a graphics frame with handles
- ◆ To adjust box style click on **Line Style** in the Graphics menu

Shading/filling

To fill a shape drawn with the rectangular, oval, circle *or* rounded corner tool
◆ Click on **Fill Style** in the Graphics menu to select from the dialogue box
◆ Select one of 36 tints *or* patterns, perimeter on *or* off, opaque *or* clear visibility and black *or* white ink
◆ Click on **Graphic** to fill the box with shading
◆ If shading has been placed over typed text then the command **Send to back** from the Page menu must be used

Text rotation

Not available

Importing pictures

◆ Click on **Import Picture** in the File menu to access the Import Picture dialogue box
◆ Select type of file from the list which includes Deluxe Paint (.LBM), Encapsulated Postscript, Gem Draw/Artline (.GEM), Gem Paint (.IMG), Lotus 123 (.PIC), PC Paintbrush (.PCX)
◆ Click on filename in Item Selector
◆ The picture name is added to the browser unless a frame is pre-selected
◆ You can only use Scale, Crop and Edit picture when a frame containing an image is selected

Cropping the picture

◆ Select picture frame
◆ Click on **Crop Picture** in the Graphics menu
◆ The mouse pointer changes to a pair of scissors
◆ Position the scissors and drag a dotted box around the portion to cut
◆ Release the mouse button and the new image will fill the frame

Scaling the picture

◆ Select picture frame
◆ Click on **Scale Picture** in the Graphics menu
◆ Click **OK** in the preserve the Aspect ratio

Editing the picture

◆ Select picture frame
◆ Click on **Edit Picture** in the Graphics menu to access a new window showing an enlarged image
◆ Click on individual pixels to toggle pixels

Sources of text ▬▬▬▬▬▬▬▬▬▬▬▬▬▬▬▬▬▬

Even though text can be typed directly in your DTP package, it is not the most efficient means of text input. Using a word processor means that the input process is not restricted to one person (the DTP operator) and also that preliminary drafts may be perfected prior to a document being imported into your publication.

Although recent releases of PageMaker and Ventura have added a search and replace facility and spell check, Timeworks does not have this facility. One of the major advantages that a word processing program has therefore is the ability to correct errors quickly and efficiently. This is one of the reasons why it is advisable to prepare your document in your word processing package, and not directly in your DTP publication.

The DTP publication on page 74 has been produced from a word processing package. The examples of these setups are laid out with paragraph and tab format characters revealed.

Basic concepts ▬▬▬▬▬▬▬▬▬▬▬▬▬▬▬▬▬▬▬▬▬▬▬▬▬▬

Certain formats are common to all DTP packages, including Timeworks, and these are explained below.

♦ Paragraph formatting should be left justified and single spaced
♦ Press **Enter** twice to start a new paragraph or line
♦ Alter tab positions in your word processor only if you want a neat draft print out. Ensure that you hit the tab only once between tabbed columns
♦ Use the Tab key not the indent key. Your paragraph styles are set in your DTP program

The following section outlines the handling of tags, and embedded codes.

Timeworks guidelines

Timeworks allows the word processing operator to insert markup codes within a document before it is imported in to Timeworks. Markup codes contain information relating to the paragraph style and some special characters such as soft hyphens and fixed spaces.

The examples on page 74 show a document prepared in a word processing program with formatting codes revealed and the final publication when imported in to your DTP program.

Tagging text

Unless otherwise tagged Timeworks styles all text as Body text when importing. Therefore, it is not necessary to tag Body text paragraphs

♦ To tag a paragraph type the style name at the start of the first line of the paragraph, enclose it in angle brackets with no preceding spaces e.g. <Headline>
♦ The paragraph style applies to all following text until Enter is pressed
♦ You cannot tag individual blocks of text within a paragraph using this method
♦ A paragraph tagged with a non-existent style name means a paragraph style will be created but with Body text attributes

Embedded codes

Timeworks can read codes placed in a wordprocessing document allowing your publication to be formatted automatically. These codes are placed within angle brackets with no spacing between the angle bracket and the code. Following are some of the codes that can be used:

<B>	Bold type begin
<N>	Return to normal
<I>	Italic begin
<S>	Small type begin
<^>	Superscript begin
<v>	Subscript begin
<189>	© symbol

Wordprocessing packages

Timeworks supports the following packages for direct import:

1st Word Plus	Displaywrite/RFT	Locoscript
Beyond WordWriter	WordPerfect 4.2	Word 4
ASCII	DCA/RFT	

If your package is not supported you can save your file as an ASCII text file and import it as such in your publication

Document set up in word processing for importing to Timeworks

<Headline>A DTP Feature ¶

¶

<Subhead>Importing Text¶

¶

Text prepared by several operators can easily and readily be read in to your Desktop Publishing package, be it <B>PageMaker, Ventura Publisher <I>or <N> <B>Timeworks Publisher<N>.¶

¶

By this means your DTP operator can receive work prepared in several different sources. Of course the criteria needs to be set prior to the WP operator starting the document. It also depends on the package as to how the details should be set up. This article illustrates basic set up only and gives examples of a few of the extensive tagging and embedded codes you can use.¶

¶

¶

<189>Lea Weston

Publication produced from word processed document

A DTP Feature

Importing Text

Text prepared by several operators can easily and readily be read in to your Desktop Publishing package, be it **PageMaker**, **Ventura Publisher** *or* **Timeworks Publisher**.

By this means your DTP operator can receive work prepared in several different sources. Of course the criteria needs to be set prior to the WP operator starting the document. It also depends on the package as to how the details should be set up. This article illustrates basic set up only and gives examples of a few of the extensive tagging and embedded codes you can use.

©Lea Weston

Character sets

Every character that you see on your screen is represented internally by a number, called its *ASCII code*. If you have graphics capability and your printer is capable of printing that character you can produce foreign-language and scientific text readily and easily.

All computer packages with the correct printer capabilities are able to print from the ASCII list. To access these additional characters you hold down the **Alt** key and type out the number using the numeric keypad. (Note that it will not work if you use the numbers across the top of the keyboard.) The diacritical marks (umlauts, tildes, etc) used in languages other than English can be inserted into an English document. For example to get the French é hold down **Alt** and type **130** on the numeric keypad. Release the **Alt** key and the é appears on the screen.

The chart on the following page indicates the standard ASCII character sets for one typeface only. Remember that you may have a number of fonts, including Symbols and Dingbats which will give you different results.

Timeworks character set

33	!	64	@	95	_	126	~	157	Ø	188	¶
34	"	65	A	96	'	127	•	158	¤	189	©
35	#	66	B	97	a	128	Ç	159	f	190	®
36	$	67	C	98	b	129	ü	160	á	191	
37	%	68	D	99	c	130	é	161	í	192	,,
38	&	69	E	100	d	131	â	162	ó	193	…
39	'	70	F	101	e	132	ä	163	ú	194	0/00
40	(	71	G	102	f	133	à	164	ñ	195	™
41	)	72	H	103	g	134	å	165	Ñ	196	–
42	*	73	I	104	h	135	ç	166	ª	197	—
43	+	74	J	105	i	136	ê	167	º	198	°
44	,	75	K	106	j	137	ë	168	¿	199	Á
45	-	76	L	107	k	138	è	169	"	200	Â
46	.	77	M	108	l	139	ï	170	"	201	É
47	/	78	N	109	m	140	î	171		202	Ê
48	0	79	O	110	n	141	ì	172		203	Ë
49	1	80	P	111	o	142	Ä	173	¡	204	Ì
50	2	81	Q	112	p	143	Å	174	«	205	Í
51	3	82	R	113	q	144	É	175	»	206	Î
52	4	83	S	114	r	145	æ	176	ã	207	Ï
53	5	84	T	115	s	146	Æ	177	õ	208	Ò
54	6	85	U	116	t	147	ô	178	¥	209	Ó
55	7	86	V	117	u	148	ö	179	¢	210	Ô
56	8	87	W	118	v	149	ò	180		211	
57	9	88	X	119	w	150	û	181		212	
58	:	89	Y	120	x	151	ù	182	À	213	Ù
59	;	90	Z	121	y	152	ÿ	183	Ã	214	Ú
60	<	91	[	122	z	153	Ö	184	Õ	215	Û
61	=	92	\	123	{	154	Ü	185	§	216	ÿ
62	>	93	]	124			155	ø	186	º	217	ß
63	?	94	^	125	}	156	£	187	»	218	/

These characters are available in Timeworks Publisher. Press and hold the **Alt** key and press the number from the number keypad. When the **Alt** key is released the character will appear.

Ventura Publisher

Introduction

Program basics
Screen layout (GEM) • Screen layout (Windows) • Help • Mouse pointer
Moving around your publication • Page view

Setting up a publication
Creating a document • Page layout • Master pages • Importing files
Direct text input • Paragraph styles • Indents • Tabs • Margins
Page numbering • Type specifications • Saving a document
Exiting Ventura

Editing a document
Retrieving a chapter • Text blocks • Editing and formatting text
Moving text • Headers and footers • Line breaks • Search and replace
Spell check • Setting up columns • Adding and deleting pages
Style sheets • Templates • Kerning • Leading • Exporting files

Printing a publication
Printing • Crop marks

Enhancements
Drawing borders and lines • Drawing boxes • Shading/filling • Text rotation
Importing pictures

Sources of text
Basic concepts • Ventura guidelines

Character sets

Ventura Publisher special characters

Introduction

Ventura Publisher is a well established office publishing product which runs on a selection of platforms: GEM, Windows or the Apple Mac. The strengths of Ventura lie in the production of long complicated documents, such as technical manuals and structured reports. Once learned it is both flexible and powerful.

Ventura Publisher copes well with sequencing and numbering chapters, figures and tables and the construction of tables of contents, indexes and cross references. Although Windows is the logical environment for Desktop Publishing on the PC the GEM version is still available and has the huge advantage of being fast.

The GEM version is able to be run on any machine from an 8086 processor upwards under DOS but Ventura Publisher 4.0 for Windows requires DOS 3.3 or higher, Windows 3, 4mb RAM and an 80286 or higher as a minimum. Even at that it makes heavy demands on your system and performance would improve with a faster processor with larger RAM.

Ventura takes a chapter based approach where style sheets, text files and graphics are referenced together but saved as separate items. It is a programme structured for the production of complex magazine and bookwork for the professional user.

To start Ventura GEM type **VP** and press **Enter** to access the program.

To start Ventura 4.0 for Windows make sure you are in Windows 3 and then double click on the **Ventura Publisher** icon.

Program basics ▬▬▬▬▬▬▬▬▬▬▬▬▬▬

Ventura Publisher screen layout (GEM) _____

Menu Bar

| Desk | File | Edit | View | Chapter | Frame | Paragraph | Graphic | Options |

```
┌──────────────────────────────────────────────────────────┐   ↑
│         │ —  │  C:\TYPESET\UNTITLRD.CHP (DEFAULT.STY)  │      │
│ ┌──┬──┬──┬──┐                                                │
│ │F │P │T │G │ ←— Mode selector                               │  ┌──┐
│ └──┴──┴──┴──┘        ┌ ─ ─ ─ ─ ─ ─ ─ ─ ─ ─ ─ ─ ─ ┐         │  │  │
│ ┌──────────┐                                         │         │  │  │
│ │Add New Tag│ ←— Addition button                               │  │  │
│ └──────────┘       │                                │         │  │V │
│ ┌──────────┐                                                  │  │e │
│ │  Body Text │       │      Screen entry area       │         │  │r │
│ │┌┐                                                   │         │  │t │
│ │││                 │                                │         │  │i │
│ │││← Assignment list                                           │  │c │
│ │││                 │                                │         │  │a │
│ │││                                                   │         │  │l │
│ │└┘                 │                                │         │  │  │
│ └──────────┘                                                  │  │S │
│ ┌──────────┐       │                                │         │  │c │
│ │          │ ←— Current selection                              │  │r │
│ ├──────────┤       └ ─ ─ ─ ─ ─ ─ ─ ─ ─ ─ ─ ─ ─ ┘         │  │o │
│ │R Pg # 0001│ ←— Page number                                  │  │l │
│ └──────────┘                                                  │  │l │
└──────────────────────────────────────────────────────────┘  └──┘
┌─┬────────────────────────────────────────────────────────┬─┐  ↓
│←│              Horizontal Scroll Bar                      │→│
└─┴────────────────────────────────────────────────────────┴─┘
```

The **Menu Bar** provides Ventura commands
The **Scroll Bars** display different parts of a document
The **Title Bar** shows the path and document name and style sheet
The **Mode selector** contains Frame, Paragraph, Text and Graphics mode
The **Addition button** displays ins, add or set depending on the mode selected
The **Assignment list** is a scrollable list of options
The **Page number** indicates the current page status
Note: Ventura Windows has no fixed side bar. Instead three movable windows - Toolbox, Tags and Files - can be placed anywhere in the work area

Ventura Publisher screen layout (Windows) _____

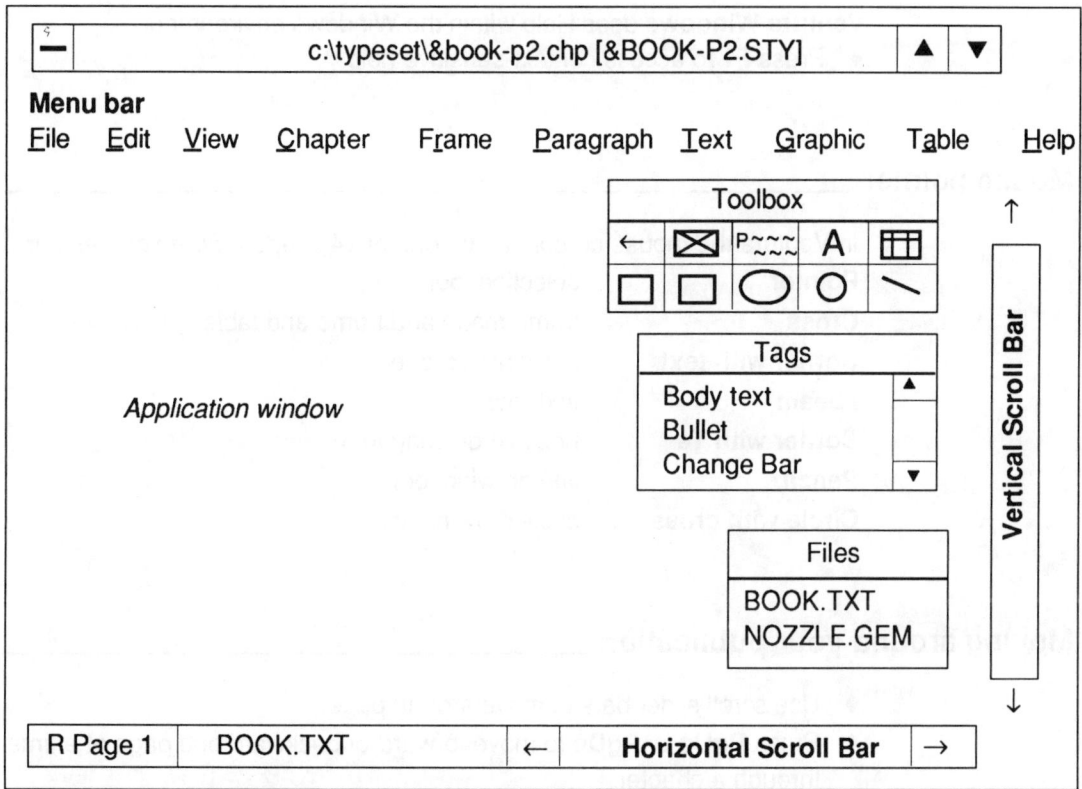

Title Bar shows the document name
Menu Bar provides Ventura Publisher commands
Scroll Bars display different parts of a document
Application window displays the working area where you create and format documents
Tags list displays the names of all tags selected and available
Files list displays in alphabetical order, the names of all files selected and available

Help

Ventura GEM provides on-screen help information as every dialogue box has a question mark box.

♦ Point to box and click and hold down the mouse button to see a list of topics

♦ Drag the cursor until selected topic is highlighted then release the mouse button

Ventura Windows uses Help within the Windows environment

♦ Press **F1** to access context-sensitive help

Mouse pointer

In Ventura the mouse cursor can be one of 14 shapes. Some of these are:

Pointer	selection tool
Cross	frame mode and frame and table
Corner with text	paragraph mode
I-beam	text tool
Corner with Te	box text drawing tool
Pencil	line drawing tool
Circle with cross	circle drawing tool

Moving around your publication

♦ Use scroll slider bars to move around page

♦ Press **PgUp** *or* **PgDn** to move forward *or* backward one page at a time through a chapter

♦ Press **Home** to move to beginning of chapter

♦ Press **End** to move to end of chapter

♦ Press **Ctrl G** to access Selected Page Field

♦ Enter page number and click **OK**

Page view

♦ Press **Ctrl R** for reduced view

♦ Press **Ctrl N** for normal view

♦ Press **Ctrl E** for enlarged view

Setting up a publication ▬▬▬▬▬▬

There are certain steps to follow when you first set up a publication in your Desktop Publishing program. The most important point to remember is to plan your document before you start. If you know what you want to achieve and draw a picture of your ideas then the end result will be worth this additional time and effort. The steps for laying out a Ventura publication are:

♦ Load a text file
♦ Load a style sheet
♦ Select and tag text as desired
♦ Add pictures
♦ Save format information
♦ Print document while it is on the screen

Creating a document ▬▬▬▬▬▬▬▬▬▬▬▬▬▬▬▬▬▬▬▬

To create a new document
♦ Click on **New** in the File menu
To name your document and create a chapter file
♦ Click on **Save As** in the File menu
♦ Complete the Item Selector Panel
♦ Click on **OK**
To load a different style sheet
♦ Click on **Load Diff.Style**
♦ Select **Style Sheet** from the list box and click **OK**

Page layout ▬▬▬▬▬▬▬▬▬▬▬▬▬▬▬▬▬▬▬▬▬▬▬▬▬▬▬▬▬▬▬▬

In Ventura the basic building block of a document is the frame which is simply a box that holds text or graphics
♦ The page itself is a frame
♦ Select **Page Size & Layout** from the Chapter menu to access Page
♦ Layout dialogue box
♦ Four options can be controlled:
Orientation: portrait or landscape
Paper type & dimensions: paper sizes
Sides: single or double
Start on: Right or left side

Master pages

The heart of Ventura is the style sheet which is a collection of information that tells Ventura how the document is to appear. For further information refer to Style Sheets section on page 91

♦ A style sheet affects four major components:
Tags controlled by Paragraph menu
Layouts controlled by Chapter menu
Frame settings controlled by the Frame menu
Printer width table

Importing files

♦ Ventura can accept text from virtually any word processor
Microsoft Word, MultiMate, WordPerfect, WordStar, Xerox Writer and XyWrite are supported directly

♦ Several word processing packages are not supported directly. These packages must be converted to *DCA Version 2.0 Revisable Form text files*: Lotus Manuscript, Displaywrite, Volkswriter, Office Writer, WordStar 2000 andSamna Word

♦ Word for Windows and Ami Professional are not yet directly supported by Ventura

To import a file

♦ Select **Load Text/Picture** from the File menu to access dialogue box
♦ Click **Text** button
♦ Click **File Format**
♦ Click **Number of files**
♦ Click **Destination**

List of Files links the file to the current chapter and appears in the Assignment List

Clipboard loads file to clipboard. The filename does not appear on the Assignment List. To load file go to **Text mode**, position cursor and press **Insert**

Cursor works same as text clipboard except position cursor BEFORE accessing **Load Text/Picture** dialogue box

♦ In Windows under Options make sure check box **Several** is not selected
♦ Click **OK**

Direct text input

♦ To enter text directly change to Text mode by clicking on **text icon**
♦ Position text I-beam cursor on the page and click
♦ Begin typing where text insertion point begins flashing
♦ On a new page the text insertion point is in the upper left corner
♦ The screen in Ventura works similarly to a word processor: text must begin in the top left hand corner

Text may be placed on the page in three ways
♦ Press **Enter** key
♦ Create a frame
♦ Format text

Paragraph styles

The key that unlocks the power of Ventura is the paragraph tag. A tag is a style template that you define and assign to one or more paragraphs in your document. Tags keep track of font settings, alignment, spacing breaks, tabs, special effects and most aspects of typography.
♦ To create a tag select **Paragraph** tool *or* press **Ctrl I**
♦ Select paragraph to tag
♦ In Ventura GEM click on **Add New Tag** addition button
♦ In Ventura Windows select **Add New Tag** from the Paragraph menu
♦ Select **Paragraph** menu to make changes as required
♦ Tag is added to the Assignment List

Indents

♦ Select **Paragraph** mode in GEM or **Paragraph** tool in Windows
♦ Select Paragraph
♦ Select **Alignment** from Paragraph menu to access Alignment dialogue box
♦ Options available are **In/Outdent Width** and **In/Outdent height**
♦ Set **Relative Indent** On
♦ To indent first line of a paragraph specify value in **In/Outdent width**
♦ To set hanging indent set **First Line** to Outdent and specify value in **In/Outdent width**
♦ To indent more than one line specify number of lines

Tabs

Because Ventura is designed so that tabs do not work in paragraphs that are justified you must change to left justify to set tabs

◆ Ventura offers four types of tabs: left, centre, right, decimal

◆ Ventura measures tab stops from the frame margin not from the edge of the page

◆ To set tabs select **Paragraph** tool and select paragraph

◆ Select **Alignment** from the Paragraph menu

◆ Select **Left Alignment** from the **Horizontal Alignment** box in the dialogue box

◆ Select **Tab Settings** from the Paragraph menu

◆ Set tabs in the Tab Settings dialogue box: Tab Number (up to 16 tabs), Tab Type (left, centre, right, decimal), Location (from margin), Leader character (spaces, dots or ASCII)

◆ Repeat tab setting criteria for each additional tab stop

◆ Click **OK**

Margins

One of the first things to do when designing a Ventura chapter is to set up the number of columns and margins of the underlying page

◆ To set margins and columns for an underlying page or frame select **Frame** mode and page or frame

◆ Select **Margins & Columns** from Frame menu to display dialogue box

◆ Select number of columns

◆ Select left or right page

◆ Set the four margins: top, bottom, left and right by typing values

◆ Click **OK**

Page numbering

To insert a page number in header or footer set up

◆ Select **Headers and Footers** from the Chapter menu to access the dialogue box

◆ Select correct set-up from the define option: left page header, right page header, left page footer, or right page footer

◆ Change Usage option to **ON**

◆ Complete left, centre or right text boxes with header or footer text if required

◆ Click on page number box and click **OK**

Type specifications

♦ Select **Text** mode
♦ Select block of text by clicking and dragging mouse

Ventura GEM

♦ Click on attribute in **Assignment List**
♦ Assignment List includes:
normal, bold, italic, small, superscript, subscript, underline, double underline, strike thru, overscore, upper case, capitalise, lower case
♦ To change font setting click the **Set Font** button

Ventura Windows

♦ Two lists are always available: the tags and files lists which are controlled from the View menu
To select attribute
♦ Click selection in **Tags List**

Saving a document

♦ Select **Save** from the File menu
♦ Complete Item Selector Panel
♦ Click **OK**
To save periodically while working on document
♦ Press **Ctrl S**
This will over-write the existing <filename>

Exiting Ventura

♦ Select **Quit** from the File menu
Before leaving you are given the chance to save or abandon the chapter and style sheet changes you made since the last save

Editing a document ▬▬▬▬▬▬▬▬▬▬▬▬

No matter how well you plan your publication before you start inevitably there are changes to be made before the document is complete. This section covers the following:

♦ Retrieving a document
♦ Text blocks
♦ Editing, formatting and moving text
♦ Headers and footers
♦ Line breaks
♦ Search and replace
♦ Spell check
♦ Setting up columns
♦ Adding/deleting pages
♦ Stylesheets/templates
♦ Kerning and leading
♦ Exporting files

Retrieving a chapter ▬▬▬▬▬▬▬▬▬▬▬▬▬▬▬▬▬▬▬▬

♦ To open a chapter click **Open** in the File menu
♦ In Ventura GEM the Item Selector appears
♦ Select document to load and click **OK**
♦ In Ventura Windows an **Open File** dialogue box appears
♦ Enter <filename> *or* select from list and click **OK**

Text blocks ▬▬▬▬▬▬▬▬▬▬▬▬▬▬▬▬▬▬▬▬▬▬▬▬▬▬▬▬

To mark a block of text
♦ Click and drag the mouse over a portion of text
♦ Text block can be deleted, copied or moved

Editing and formatting text _____

- ◆ Click on **Text** mode
- ◆ Position cursor and click
- ◆ Ventura always operates in text mode
- ◆ To delete single letters or small amounts of text place the cursor in front of text to delete and press **Delete** key
- ◆ To delete text to the left of the cursor press **Backspace** key
- ◆ To delete blocks of text select text then press **Delete** *or* select **Cut Text** from the Edit menu

Moving text _____

To move text
- ◆ Select the text
- ◆ Press **Delete** *or* select **Cut Text** from the Edit menu
- ◆ Position text cursor in new position
- ◆ Press **Insert** *or* select **Paste Text** from the Edit menu

Headers and footers _____

- ◆ Ventura offers the options of inserting headers or footers on every page, all odd pages, all even pages or selected pages
- ◆ Different headers can be set up on odd and even pages
- ◆ Each line of header or footer is limited to 57 characters including attributes
- ◆ Two lines are the limit for each left, centre or right footer or header
- ◆ Select **Headers and Footers** from the Chapter menu to access the dialogue box
- ◆ Select correct set-up from the define option: left page header, right page header, left page footer, or right page footer
- ◆ Change Usage option to **ON**
- ◆ Complete left, centre or right blanks with header or footer text if required
- ◆ Click **OK**

Line breaks

A break is when a blank line is inserted in text. A line break does not create a paragraph
- Press **Ctrl Enter** at text cursor position to move text to next line
- To access the **Breaks** dialogue box change to **Paragraph** tool select a paragraph and select **Breaks** from the Paragraph menu

Search and replace

Not available in GEM but available in the Windows environment
To perform a search and replace in Windows
- Select page frame
- Select **Search and replace** option from Edit menu to access the dialogue box
- Choose **Text Atributes** or **Tags** option
- Enter details in **Search For** box
- Enter details in **Replace with** box
- Follow commands and make selections as required i.e. replace skip etc
- When search is complete select **OK** to end

Spell check

Not available in GEM but available in the Windows environment
- Select **Spell check** from the Edit menu

Setting up columns

- To set up columns for an underlying page change to **Frame** mode and select the page or frame
- Select **Margins & Columns** from Frame menu to access Margins and Columns dialogue box
- Click from 1 to 8 to select number of columns
- The number of columns is divided into Actual Frame Width minus Left and Right margins to produce columns of equal width
- Each column can have a custom width
- To obtain columns of unequal width edit the widths manually
- The default gutter space (space between columns) is 0
- Enter the amount in **Gutters** column to amend the default setting
- Click **OK**

Adding and deleting pages

♦ Select **Insert/Remove Page** from Chapter menu to access dialogue box
♦ Options include: insert new page before current page, insert new page after current page, or remove current page
♦ Add number of pages
♦ Click **OK**

Style sheets

In Ventura when you set up a new publication you create three defaults: Chapter, Frame and Style sheet. As previously stated a style sheet affects four major components: **tags**, **layouts**, **frame settings** and **printer width table**. One great strength of Ventura is the ability to quickly change the entire design of a chapter by switching style sheets

♦ When you load a chapter the style sheet assigned to that chapter is also loaded
♦ DEFAULT.STY is loaded when Ventura is first loaded
♦ Default style sheet contains no paragraph tags other than Body text tag
♦ To name a style sheet select **Save As New Style** from File menu
♦ In the dialogue box enter style sheet name
♦ Ventura adds the .STY extension
♦ Click **OK**
♦ To load a style sheet select **Load Diff.Style** from the File menu
♦ In the dialogue box enter style sheet name *or* select from list
♦ Click **OK**

Templates

Ventura Publisher provides a number of template style sheets from which you can create your own documents.

The style sheets are setup ready to use if they have been copied to your computer system.

The Ventura Publisher style sheets are in a sub-directory called VP Style. Remember, that you must rename the style sheets if you make changes or you will lose the original samples.

To retain sample sheets
- ♦ Load the chapter
- ♦ Delete any text file and illustrations
- ♦ Select **Save As New Style** and give style sheet a new name
- ♦ Select **Save As** and give a new chapter name

The designs include a wide variety of the features included in Ventura Publisher and may enhance your design capabilities and add to your Desktop Publishing presentations.

The 52 Ventura Publisher sample style sheets fall into various categories and include a variety of designs and chapters. Listed below are the file names, all with the extension .chp e.g. Newslttr.chp and the categories they include:

Academic
Newslttr, Thesis, Txtbook

Advertising Materials
Ad, Q&A, Brochure, Invite, Flyer, Sign

Business Documents
Memo, Proposal, Release, Orgchart, Qtrrpt, Fax, Letter, Envelope, Award, B-Cards, Resume, Label

Database Publishing
Catalog, Partslst, Pricelst, Phonelst

Financial
Balsheet, 10kreprt, Inspolcy

Forms
Invoice, Purchord, Calendar, Time-man

Government
Milspec, Policy

Long Documents
Techdoc, Book, Book2, Manual, Magartcl, Index, TOC, TOC-2

News Reporting
Nletter, Scoop, Journal, Tabloid

Word Presentation
Presport, Preslan

Vertical Applications
Contract, Legalbrf, Depositi, Spec

Kerning

Kerning makes the spacing between letters tighter or looser by a specified amount. Ventura Publisher allows kerning *either* manually *or* automatically. Automatic kerning controls have no effect on manual kerning and vice versa

♦ For kerning to be active set **Pair Kerning ON** in the Chapter Typographical box in the Chapter menu

To adjust kerning

♦ Select text to adjust
♦ Press **Ctrl 2** to access **Select Font Setting** for Selected text

To kern text visually

♦ Select a single letter, press **Shift Right Arrow** *or* **Shift Left Arrow** to loosen *or* tighten the space

Leading

Vertical spacing (leading) is the spacing between lines of text

♦ Select paragraph tool and select a paragraph
♦ Select **Spacing** from the Paragraph menu to access Spacing dialogue box
♦ Changes can be made to:
   Inter-line spacing (leading: Ventura calculates at 1.2 times the point size i.e. a 10 point type size equals 12 point leading)
   Above: default is set by Ventura to same value as leading
   Below: Adds space after a paragraph
   Inter-paragraph: only calculated if above and below values are identical

Exporting files

Ventura's renaming function can be used to convert files from one word processing format to another

Convert text files from any format Ventura supports to any other format

♦ Ensure file is loaded in Ventura
♦ In **Frame** mode click page or frame
♦ Select **File Type/Rename** from the Edit menu
♦ Select path and enter <filename>
♦ Select text format
♦ Click **OK**

Printing a publication ▬▬▬▬▬▬▬

Printing a publication is ultimately what Desktop Publishing is all about. The end product of all your efforts - the concrete evidence of your labour, your writing and editing, your graphics capability and your design skills - is the printed sheet(s) of paper.

Printing ───────────────────────────────

♦ Select **Print** from the File menu to access the Print Information dialogue box
♦ Complete the items in the dialogue box:
  All, Selected, Left, Right, Current
♦ Define no. of copies (max no. is 999)
♦ Complete options
♦ Click **OK**

Crop marks ─────────────────────────────

♦ Select **ON** from Print dialogue box to insert crop marks used by typesetters to line up pages

Enhancements ▬▬▬▬▬▬▬▬▬▬▬▬▬

Once your document has been setup the benefits of Desktop Publishing are the ease with which enhancements such as graphics, boxes and tables can be added to your text. This section covers:

♦ Drawing borders and lines
♦ Drawing boxes
♦ Special effects: shading/filling
♦ Text rotation
♦ Importing pictures

Drawing borders and lines _____

♦ Select **Graphics** mode
♦ Select **Drawing** tool
♦ Select **straight line** icon to draw a line
♦ Click and hold mouse down
♦ Drag mouse to where line should finish
♦ To ensure line is straight hold the **Alt** key down while drawing line
♦ To adjust line style, thickness and end style line click on **Line Attributes** in the Graphics menu

Drawing boxes _____

♦ Select **Graphics** mode
♦ Click on **Rectangle** drawing tool to draw a box
♦ Click and hold mouse button down and drag to size and position of box
♦ To draw a square rather than a rectangle hold the **Alt** key down while drawing the box
♦ To adjust line style and thickness click on **Line Attributes** in the Graphics menu

Box text

♦ Select **Graphics** mode
♦ Click on **Box Text**
♦ Pull box to size required and then key in text
♦ The box text tag can be altered if required
♦ If text does not fit in the box highlight the box click and extend as required

Shading/fill _____

- Select graphic and select **Fill Attributes** from the Graphics menu to access the Fill Attributes dialogue box for the type of graphic object
- Separate dialogue boxes are available for the Box Text, circle, rectangle and rounded rectangle options
- Change colour or pattern
- Click **OK**

Text rotation _____

- Text rotation affects the entire paragraph
- Text rotation is limited to 90 degree increments only
- To set up text rotation create a paragraph tag
- Select **Alignment** from the Paragraph menu to access Alignment dialogue box
- Select degree of rotation: 90, 180 and 270
- Click **OK**

Importing pictures _____

Ventura Publisher uses frames to hold pictures just as it uses frames to hold text. When you load a picture into a frame you can place the frame anywhere on the page. Wherever you locate a frame the text already in place flows around the picture in the frame

- Select **Load Text/Picture** from the File menu to access dialogue box
- Select one of two kinds of pictures: Line Art *or* Image
- Line Art box presents these format choices: GEM, Windows Metafile, AutoCad.SLD, Lotus.PIC, VideoShow, MacPICT, CGM, Postscript, HPGL Image box presents these format choices: GEM/Halo.DPE, PCX, MacPaint, TIFF
- Click **OK** to access Item Selector dialogue box
- Click Graphics filename
- Click **OK**
- If an empty frame is selected the picture is loaded into that frame Otherwise the name of the picture appears in the **Assignment List**

Scaling a picture

♦ Controls the size of the graphic inside the frame

♦ Also can control the aspect ratio which determines whether an image looks distorted or normally proportioned

♦ Select Frame mode and select **Sizing & Scaling** from the Frame menu to access dialogue box

♦ Each element has two options thus four possible combinations: Scaling by Fit in Frame or By Scale factors; Aspect Ratio by Maintained or Distorted

Cropping the picture

Cropping does not change the size of the picture; the picture's relationship to the frame is changed

♦ To enlarge or shrink a picture without changing the frame size use the **Sizing and Scaling** dialogue box

♦ To visually crop a picture press and hold the **Alt** key and press the mouse button in frame or graphic mode

♦ The cursor becomes a small hand that can push the picture left, right, up or down in the frame

Sources of text ▬▬▬▬▬▬▬▬▬▬▬▬▬▬▬▬

Even though text can be typed directly in your DTP package, it is not the most efficient means of text input.   Using a word processor means that the input process is not restricted to one person (the DTP operator) and also that preliminary drafts can be perfected prior to the text being imported into your publication.

Although Ventura now has a search and replace facility and spell check, one of the major advantages that a word processing program has is the ability to correct errors quickly and efficiently. This is one of the reasons why it is advisable to prepare your document in your word processing package, and not directly in to your DTP publication.

In Ventura the word processing programs accepted will depend upon the filters set up at installation. An assumption has been made that all filters available for your program have been installed.

The DTP publication on page 101 has been produced from a word processing package. The example of this setup is laid out with paragraph and tab format characters revealed for each program.

Basic concepts ▬▬▬▬▬▬▬▬▬▬▬▬▬▬▬▬▬▬▬▬▬▬▬

There are certain formats that are common to all packages and these are explained below.
♦ Paragraph formatting should be left justified and single spaced
♦ Unless a double space is required between paragraphs press **Enter** only once
♦ Alter tab positions in your word processor only if you want a neat draft print out. Ensure that you hit the tab only once between tabbed columns
♦ Use the tab key not the indent key. Your paragraph styles are set in your DTP program
Following is a section which outlines the handling of tags, and embedded codes.

Ventura guidelines

Ventura creates typeset documents from text prepared and setup in your word processors. Codes embedded in your document allow tags, non-keyboard characters, tabs, text attributes and other inserted text to be read directly in to your publication.

The example on page 101 shows a word processing document set up to produce the typeset document in the example underneath it

Tags

♦ Undefined tags in Timeworks are treated as Body text tags

♦ To tag a paragraph use the @ sign and the style name at the start of a line followed by an equal sign. The @ must be the first character in the line at the beginning of the paragraph e.g. @Headline=

♦ Tags apply to all following text until you press Enter
A paragraph tagged with an undefined tag will be treated as Body text

Embedding codes

Ventura reads embedded codes which are enclosed in angle brackets directly in to your publication.

Text attribute commands have some formatting specifications

♦ Several attributes can be combined within one set of angle brackets e.g. <BIP14> is bold, italic type 14 point size

♦ All attributes are turned off at the end of a paragraph *or* when you insert <D>

♦ All attributes are turned off when another attribute command is encountered

Following are some of the more frequently used codes:

<B>	Bold
<D>	Return to normal
<U>	Underline
<I>	Italics
<N>	Non-breaking space
<S>	Small type
<^>	Superscript
<v>	Subscript

You can also insert non-keyboard characters such as <189> to produce ©

Word processing packages

Ventura supports the following packages for direct import:

WordStar 3.3 and 3.4

WordStar 4 and 5.x

WordPerfect

WordPerfect 5

XyWrite

Word

Word for Windows

MultiMate

Writer

ASCII

DCA

Notes

Word and Word for Windows

♦ Ventura will not accept Word or Word for Windows style sheets

WordPerfect

♦ 4.1 and 4.2 can be read using the WordPerfect 4 option

♦ Use WordPerfect 5 to load version 5.x files

♦ WordPerfect 5.1 users save in the 5.0 format before importing into Ventura

Document set up in word processing for importing to Ventura

@Headline=A DTP Feature ¶
¶
@Subhead=Importing Text¶
¶
Text prepared by several operators can easily and readily be read in to your
Desktop Publishing package, be it <B>PageMaker, Ventura Publisher <I>or
<D> <B>Timeworks Publisher<D>.¶
By this means your DTP operator can receive work prepared in several
different sources . Of course the criteria needs to be set prior to the WP
operator starting the document. It also depends on the package as to how the
details should be set up. This article illustrates basic set up only and gives
examples of a few of the extensive tagging and embedded codes you can
use.¶
¶
¶
<189>Lea Weston

Publication produced from word processed document

A DTP Feature

Importing Text

Text prepared by several operators can easily and readily be read in to
your Desktop Publishing package, be it **PageMaker**, **Ventura Publisher** *or*
Timeworks Publisher.

By this means your DTP operator can receive work prepared in several
different sources. Of course the criteria needs to be set prior to the WP
operator starting the document. It also depends on the package as to how
the details should be set up. This article illustrates basic set up only and
gives examples of a few of the extensive tagging and embedded codes you
can use.

©Lea Weston

Character sets

Every character that you see on your screen is represented internally by a number, called its *ASCII code*. If you have graphics capability and your printer is capable of printing that character you can produce foreign-language and scientific text readily and easily.

All computer packages with the correct printer capabilities are able to print from the ASCII list. To access these additional characters you hold down the **Alt** key and type out the number using the numeric keypad. (Note that it will not work if you use the numbers across the top of the keyboard.) The diacritical marks (umlauts, tildes, etc) used in languages other than English can be inserted into an English document. For example to get the French é hold down **Alt** and type **130** on the numeric keypad. Release the **Alt** key and the é appears on the screen.

Under the Windows environment additional characters and symbols are available in the same manner. To insert these characters you type in a four digit number, rather than the three for ASCII. The method remains the same, i.e. press **Alt 0233** for the French é.

The chart on the following page indicates the standard ASCII character sets for one typeface only. Remember that you may have a number of fonts, including Symbols and Dingbats which will give you different results. In addition, you will find the ANSI codes slightly different from the Ventura Publisher ASCII codes.

Ventura Publisher character set

033	!	063	?	093	]	0123	{	0191	¿	0223	ß
034	"	064	@	094	^	0124	|	0192	À	0224	à
035	#	065	A	095	_	0125	}	0193	Á	0225	á
036	$	066	B	096	`	0126	~	0194	Â	0226	â
037	%	067	C	097	a			0195	Ã	0227	ã
038	&	068	D	098	b	0132	„	0196	Ä	0228	ä
039	'	069	E	099	c	0133	…	0197	Å	0229	å
040	(	070	F	0100	d			0198	Æ	0230	æ
041	)	071	G	0101	e	0136	ƒ	0199	Ç	0231	ç
042	*	072	H	0102	f			0200	È	0232	è
043	+	073	I	0103	g	0147	"	0201	É	0233	é
044	,	074	J	0104	h	0148	"	0202	Ê	0234	ê
045	-	075	K	0105	i			0203	Ë	0235	ë
046	.	076	L	0106	j	0150	–	0204	Ì	0236	ì
047	/	077	M	0107	k	0151	—	0205	Í	0237	í
048	0	078	N	0108	l	0153	™	0206	Î	0238	î
049	1	079	O	0109	m			0207	Ï	0239	ï
050	2	080	P	0110	n	0162	¢				
051	3	081	Q	0111	o	0163	£	0209	Ñ	0241	ñ
052	4	082	R	0112	p	0167	§	0210	Ò	0242	ò
053	5	083	S	0113	q	0169	©	0211	Ó	0243	ó
054	6	084	T	0114	r			0212	Ô	0244	ô
055	7	085	U	0115	s	0170	ª	0213	Õ	0245	õ
056	8	086	V	0116	t	0171	«	0214	Ö	0246	ö
057	9	087	W	0117	u	0176	°				
058	:	088	X	0118	v			0216	Ø	0248	ø
059	;	089	Y	0119	w	0182	¶	0217	Ù	0249	ù
060	<	090	Z	0120	x	0186	º	0218	Ú	0250	ú
061	=	091	[	0121	y	0187	»	0219	Û	0251	û
062	>	092	\	0122	z			0220	Ü	0252	ü
										0255	ÿ

These ANSI characters are available in Ventura Publisher. Press and hold the **Alt** key and press the number from the number keypad. When the **Alt** key is released the character will appear.

Ventura Publisher special characters _____

Item	Key combination
Copyright sign	**Ctrl Shift C**
Disc hyphen	**Ctrl -**
Em dash	**Ctrl]**
Em space	**Ctrl Shift M**
En space	**Ctrl Shift N**
En dash	**Ctrl [**
Figure space	**Ctrl Shift F**
Non-breaking space	**Ctrl space**
Quote, Open "	**Ctrl Shift [**
Quote, Closed "	**Ctrl Shift]**
Registered trademark	**Ctrl Shift R**
Thin space	**Ctrl Shift T**
Trademark	**Ctrl Shift 2**

Examples

DTP programs are well suited to the task of setting up columns for producing newsletters, advertisements, manuals etc. They do it with much more ease and visibility than the wordprocessing packages which include columns as part of their set up. Deciding on the exact number of columns to use will depend on a variety of factors.

It is wise to remember to make your document have the look and feel typical of the type of publication you are creating e.g. a newspaper would be hard to read as a single A4 column, similarly a number of columns would not be suitable for a simple report.

The guidelines below may help you to decide the number of columns you will need:

Reports	1 column
Newsletters	2 or 3 columns
Newspapers	3 or 4 columns
Magazines	1 to 4 columns
Books	1 or 2 columns
Manuals	1 or 2 columns

Reminder: as you increase the number of columns on a page, from the point of view of appearance and readability, it is best to decrease the text point size. Thus, the most efficient way of putting more words onto a page is to increase the number of columns. To merely reduce the type size on a single page layout would make your publication hard to read.

On the following pages we will create a 3-column newsletter in each of the DTP packages included in this Guide.

Creating a newsletter in PageMaker _____

The PageMaker approach to creating a newsletter with multiple columns is easy. The procedures are those which can be used for producing any type of publication. The master page, which is the foundation for any publication created in PageMaker, will be set up to ensure a consistent look for the entire publication.

To set up a newsletter

♦ Select **New** from the File menu
♦ Select **Save As** and name the file
♦ Adjust settings in the Page Setup dialogue box and click OK
♦ From the Edit menu select **Preferences** to check the options and click OK
♦ Double check that Rulers, Toolbox and Scroll Bars are visible on screen
♦ Click the **Master Page** icon to select the master page

To create columns

♦ From the Options menu select **Column guides**
♦ Type **3** for number of columns
♦ *Either* accept the default space between columns or tab to this box and type a space figure
♦ Click OK

To position the ruler guides

♦ Zoom to 200% size to allow precision when placing ruler guides
♦ Select **Snap to rulers** from the Options menu
♦ Place the cursor on the horizontal ruler and holding down the mouse button drag a ruler guide to position on the vertical ruler
♦ Point inside the vertical ruler and drag the ruler guide to position on the horizontal ruler
♦ Select **Lock guides** form the Options menu

Tip: It is a good idea to save your work as you go along so that any mistakes made can be altered from the last point of saving. To do this press **Ctrl S** and it will save the named file

To draw borders

♦ Check that Snap to guides from the Options menu is checked
♦ Select either the **Square corner** tool or the **Rounded corner** tool from the toolbox
♦ Select **Line** from the Element menu and define thickness of the line
♦ Point to where the ruler guides intersect in the upper left corner and drag to position in the right corner
♦ Draw a second and third border if required

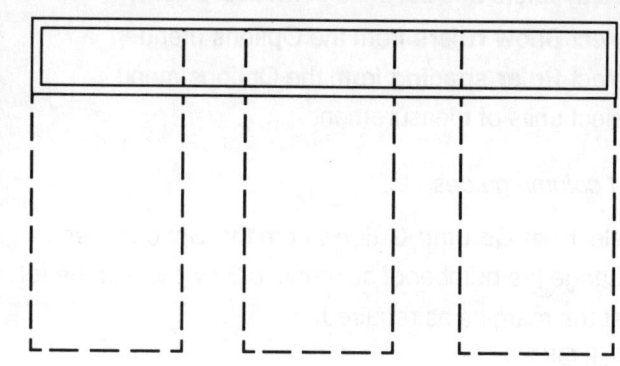

To create a text footer and add a page number
♦ Drag a ruler guide down to position
♦ Define Type specs from the Type menu
♦ Enter text for the footer if required
♦ Press **Ctrl** + **Shift** + **C** to centre text *or* **Ctrl** + **Shift** + **R** to align right
♦ Press **Ctrl** + **Shift** + **3** to insert the page number character

Now that the master page has been set up work can be started on the newsletter
♦ Build the newsletter heading
♦ Place text and/or graphics on the page

Note:

When you place text on a page PageMaker looks for a column to flow the text into. When it can't find a column it flows the text between the margins. To place text within margins or column guides clicking the loaded text icon is the easiest method. But there may be occasions when you want to indent the text from the left column guide and the right margin to leave space for a box. Then, drag-placing is the answer. Set up ruler guides and drag the text within any boundaries you set.
♦ The last thing to remember is SAVE YOUR WORK as you go along

Creating a newsletter in Timeworks

In Timeworks the first step in the process of setting up a newsletter is to determine the basic requirements for the master page

To start a new publication
♦ Select **New** from the File menu
♦ Select **Save** and name the file
♦ Select **No** when asked to load a stylesheet
♦ Select paper size, pages alike and paper orientation
♦ Select **Go to page** in the Page menu and select **Go to Master Page**

To display rulers and set units of measurement

♦ Select **Show rulers** from the Options menu
♦ Select **Ruler spacing** from the Options menu
♦ Select units of measurement

To set column guides

♦ Select **Set Column Guides** from the Options menu
♦ Change the number of columns to 3 by clicking the **left arrow** 3 times
♦ Set the margins as required
♦ Click OK

To set up footer and page number

♦ Select **Page numbers** from the Text menu and select numbering
♦ Select **Headers and footers** from the Text menu
♦ Complete dialogue box with information
♦ Click OK

To set frames

♦ Select **frame** tool and drag out the first frame to cover the left hand column
♦ Set the frame background
♦ Copy this frame twice by selecting **Copy** from the Edit menu and then **Paste** from the Edit menu
♦ Drag the copies onto the centre and right hand columns
♦ Set masthead frame

To place text or graphics in the frames

♦ Using the **Frame** tool highlight the first column on the page
♦ Select **Import text** from the File menu and select format
♦ Double click on import document name and text flows to highlighted frame
♦ To place left over text, highlight other frames in turn and select document name in the Browser
♦ Format text as per style guidelines set
Reminder:
♦ Save your work as you go along

Creating a newsletter in Ventura Publisher

A newsletter chapter can contain multiple articles each saved in a different text file. These articles can start on any page and can continue on any later page. Each portion of each article can be placed in a frame anywhere in the chapter. Each frame can have its own set of margin column and vertical rule settings. You can generate complete layouts by placing text into frames rather than directly onto a page.

To compose a newsletter layout:
♦ Load a style sheet similar to the format you want to produce or load default.sty style sheet
♦ From File menu select **SaveAs** and type a style sheet name
♦ From File menu load any text or picture files
♦ Select **Selection** tool
♦ From Chapter menu select **page size** and **layout option** and change orientation and paper type and dimension
♦ From File menu select **Save** to save the file with the same name as the placed text file with the extension .CHP. (Select Save As option to rename the chapter)
♦ If necessary from the Chapter menu change the Chapter Typography settings
♦ Select the page then modify margins, ruling lines and frame background for the page. These changes will affect every page in the document
♦ From the Frame menu select **Margins and Columns** and enter 3 columns
♦ From the View menu enable the **Show Column Guides** option to display guides on the screen. The column settings provide a grid to align the separate frames which you manually draw

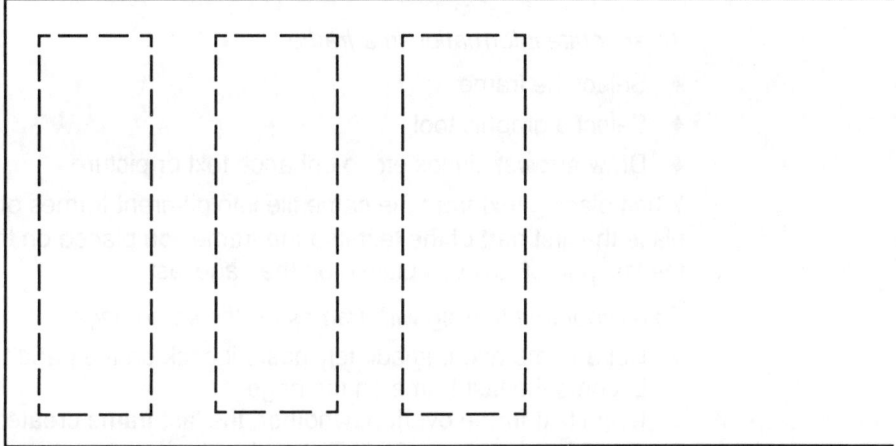

♦ Use the **Add Frame** tool to create frames where text is to appear

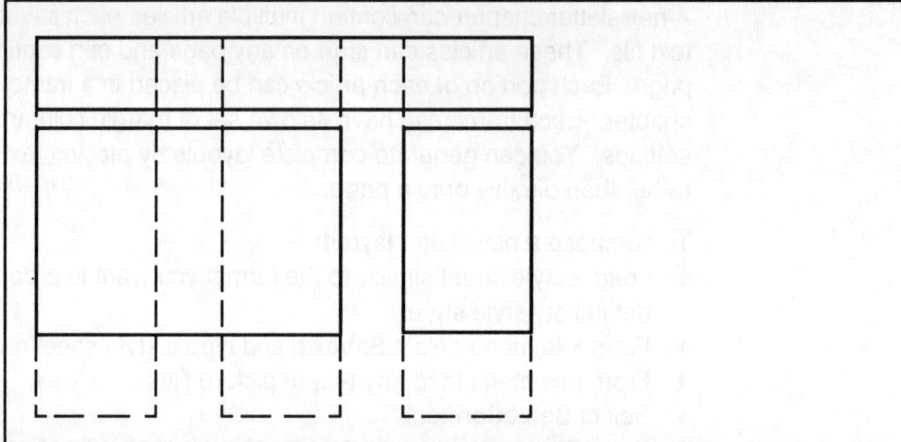

♦ Place text or pictures into each frame. To place text in a frame select the frame then select file name from the Files list
♦ Increase or decrease frame size to be able to change text it contains; position frame where you want it
♦ Select Chapter menu **Insert/Remove Page** to insert new page

To continue text into a new frame from a previous frame

♦ Select new frame
♦ Select text file name in Files list to continue text from previous frame
Note that text cannot be made to flow to a previous page
♦ Amend frame attributes as necessary using **Options** in the Frame menu

Tips

To annotate information in a frame

♦ Select the frame
♦ Select a graphic tool
♦ Draw arrows, circles etc to enhance text or picture
When placing text from the same file into different frames on the same page place the first part of the text into the frame you placed on the page first and the last part of text you placed on the page last

To reorder text flowing with frames on the same page

♦ Cut a frame and immediately paste it back on the page to have this frame become the last frame on the page
♦ If one text frame overlaps another, the last frame created appears on top of the first frame created. The text in the bottom frame flows around the frame on top

New pages are not created automatically

Appendix

Although using the mouse is an integral part of these menu driven DTP programs, there are still some keyboard shortcuts which will speed certain moves for you. For example, press **Ctrl S** in any one of the packages to save a file which has already been named. Caution: pressing **Ctrl S** could overwrite your default file. To start with it might be easier to use **Save As** from the File menu.

Ventura Publisher and PageMaker use the **Ctrl** key in combination with a letter or number but Timeworks uses the **Alt** key. As the listing on page 113 demonstrates, PageMaker has made greater use of the function keys than the other two.

This section contains four useful information categories:
♦ Speed and function key combinations
♦ ASCII characters
♦ Hints and tips on designing a document
♦ Glossary of DTP terms

Speed keys

	Ventura GEM Ctrl +	Ventura Windows Ctrl +	PageMaker Ctrl +	Timeworks Alt +
A	Bring to front	Bring to front	Select all (Edit menu)	Repeat search
B	Renumber chapter	Renumber chapter	Send to back	Bold on/off
C	Insert special item	-	-	Copy
D	Edit special item	Edit special item	Place file	-
E	Enlarged screen view	Enlarged screen view	Edit story	Show frames & columns
F	Fill attributes	Fill attributes	Bring to front	Search text
G	GoTo page	GoTo page	GoTo page	GoTo page
H	-	-	Hyphenation	Show tools
I	Paragraph mode	Paragraph tool	Indents/tabs	Italics
J	-	-	Guides	Show rulers
K	Assign further keys	Update tag list	Colour palette	Kern
L	Line attributes	Line attributes	Spell check	Light text
M	-	-	Paragraph	Switch modes
N	Normal screen view	Normal screen view	New file	Normal text
O	Text mode	Text tool	Open file	Open file

	Ventura GEM Ctrl +	Ventura Windows Ctrl +	PageMaker Ctrl +	Timeworks Alt +
P	Graphic drawing	Table tool	Print file	Print file
Q	Select all (graphics mode)	Select all graphics	Exit	Quit
R	Reduced screen view	Reduced screen view	Rulers	Search & replace
S	Save file	Save file	Save file	Save
T	Show/hide tabs & returns	Show/hide tabs & returns	Type specifications	Font & size
U	Frame mode	Frame tool	Snap to guides	Underline
V	-	Show/hide tag list window	-	Paste
W	Show/hide side bar	Show/hide toolbox	Fit in window	White text
X	Recall last menu box displayed	Recall last dialogue box	-	Cut
Y	-	Show/hide File List window	Style palette	-
Z	Send to back	Send to back	-	Hide all pictures

	Ventura GEM Ctrl +	Ventura Windows Ctrl +	PageMaker Ctrl +	Timeworks Alt +
0		-	25% display size	Half size
1		-	Actual display size	3/4 size
2	Font setting selected text	Font setting selected text	200% display size	Actual size
3			Define styles	Double size
4			400% display size	Full page
5			50% display size	2 pages
6			Toolbox	Bring to front
7			75% display size	Send to back
8			Find from Edit menu	-
9			Change from Edit menu	-
+				Superscript
-				Subscript

Function keys ▬▬▬▬▬▬▬▬▬▬▬▬▬▬▬▬

	Ventura GEM Ctrl +	Ventura Windows Ctrl +	PageMaker Ctrl +	Timeworks Alt +
F1	Help	Help	Help index	Body text
F2	}	{	-	Headline
F3	}	{	-	Bullet
F4	} Free to assign	{	-	Subhead
F5	} as tag names	{	Normal type	
F6	}	{	Bold type	
F7	}	{	Italic type	
F8	}	{	Underline type	
F9	}	{	Pointer tool	
F10	Body text	{		
Shift F2			Diagonal line tool	
Shift F3			Perpendicular line tool	
Shift F4			Text tool	
Shift F5			Square corner tool	
Shift F6			Rounded corner tool	
Shift F7			Oval tool	
Shift F8			Cropping tool	

Hints and tips

The purpose of graphic design is to make it as easy as possible for readers to understand your message. Graphic design is a tool, not an end in itself. Success is measured in the speed and ease with which ideas are communicated to the reader.

There are certain guidelines which can be adapted to most situations to provide a framework for your design approach.

♦ Be willing to experiment
♦ Be flexible in applying rules
♦ Be consistent
♦ Do not try to create a design style
♦ Avoid static balance
♦ Utilise a single dominant visual element
♦ Concentrate your design in terms of facing pages
♦ Format publications for easy transition from section to section
♦ Create a grid
♦ Standardise margins
♦ Use borders
♦ Organise copy into columns
♦ Use horizontal and vertical rules
♦ Use headers and footers for information
♦ Use type to create identity
♦ Balance mastheads and headlines
♦ Use subheads to provide transition from headline to body copy
♦ Use captions
♦ Use colour to add a difference
♦ Use large type or vary type styles to emphasize important ideas
♦ Use reverse type to add emphasis to headlines
♦ Use shading to attract attention
♦ Use boxes to emphasize text or graphics
♦ Illustrate with graphics
♦ Pay attention to detail, check for text and layout mistakes

- ◆ Adjust line spacing
- ◆ Watch out for widows and orphans
- ◆ Adjust letter spacing with kerning
- ◆ Adjust word spacing with hyphens
- ◆ Pay attention to punctuation

Four steps to success

1 Plan your project
2 Establish a format
3 Add emphasis where needed
4 Check and re-check your work

Glossary of DTP terms

Alignment	The way elements are laid out on a page
Anchored	Fixed or attached to a point on the page in the publication window
ASCII Text	Acronym for American Standard Code for Information Interchange - provides a common computer code to represent letters and numbers
Aspect ratio	The relationship between the height and width of an image when it is displayed on screen or printed out
Attributes	A style given to text for effect and readability, such as italics, fonts and point size
Autoflow	A mode of text placement in which text flows continuously onto successive pages or columns
Baseline	An imaginary line along the bottom edge of capital letters
Binding margin	Extra space added to the side of a printed page to allow for punching or binding: usually the left-hand side of a right page and the right-hand side of a left page
Body text	The main text of a document
Browser	A list of all the text files, drawn pictures and scans which have been imported into the document
Bullet	A heavy dot or other symbol used as an ornament before a paragraph and in lists
Clipboard	A temporary holding place for a block of text, a frame, or a graphic which has been copied

Column guides	Dotted lines only visible on screen which can be used to help position frames on the page
Crop	To mask unwanted areas of an image
Crop marks	Marks on film or camera ready artwork to indicate the outside edge of the page, to which it will be trimmed
Default	An option or setting that a program automatically uses unless otherwise specified
Em	A unit for measuring width which is equivalent to the point size of the font in question
Em rule	Used in typography to represent the dash punctuation mark
Em space	The width of the letter M in the current point size
En	A unit for measuring width usually half the width of the em and equivalent to the width of a lowercase n
Fixed space	A space used to keep words together on the same line which is never stretched during justification
Font	A complete set of characters of the same design style and relative size
Frame	A rectangular box used to hold text, pictures or graphics
GEM	A Digital Research graphical interface between the user and the computer's operating system
Grabber hand	The icon that appears in place of the pointer to move the page around a publication window
Graphics grid	A piece of 'graph paper' within a graphics frame. With *Snap to grid* turned on, graphics are aligned to the grid points on this graph paper when they are drawn or moved

Greeking	A method of representing text by a series of horizontal lines used when text is too small to display legibly
Gutter space	The distance between columns
Handles	Small open squares on the edges and corners of a selected frame or graphic which are used for sizing
Hanging indent	A paragraph style where the first line is flush with the left margin and subsequent lines are indented
Hairline	A very thin line
Icon	Image used by a computer application which can be opened by clicking the mouse
Image	A picture represented on screen and printed as a series of dots or bit map
Kerning	Adjusting the spacing between pairs of characters to create a more pleasing effect and save space
Leading	The distance from the baseline of a line of text to the next
Line Art	A picture reproduced (or produced) by computer from a mathematically defined object: anything that is not bit mapped
Markup language	A series of codes representing typesetting information (such as paragraph style) that can be inserted into text using a word processor before importing it
Master page	A single or double sided page which acts as a template for any new pages added to a document
Monospacing	A method of spacing characters where each character occupies the same amount of horizontal space

Orientation	The position of a page, either landscape or portrait
Orphan	The first line of a paragraph situated at the bottom of a column or page, separated from the rest of the paragraph in the following column or page
Padding	The space around a frame which text cannot overlap, usually called standoff
Page format	The arrangement of text, pictures and graphics on a page
Pantone	A colour system of over 700 standard colours developed by Pantone Inc and used by designers, ink manufacturers and commercial printers
Paragraph style	The name for a particular type of paragraph with its own set of features e.g. font, point size, bullets and indents
Pasteboard	The work surface surrounding the page(s) you are working on. Text and graphics remain there when you turn to another page or close the publication
Pica	A typesetting unit of measurement equal to 1/6 of an inch
Point	A typesetting unit of measurement equal to 1/72 of an inch
Point size	The height of a font measured in points
Polyline	A curved line made up of straight line segments
Proportional spacing	A means of spacing characters whereby the space each character occupies varies according to the width of the character e.g. the letter i occupies less space than the letter m
Repel text	To make text run around the outside of a frame
Reverse video	With black and white reversed; so that white characters are displayed on a black background

Rivers	The excessive spaces in justified text which join together to form white rivers running through paragraphs of text
Roman text	Plain text characterised by upgirth letters of normal thickness
Rulers	Electronic rulers: horizontal is displayed across the top of the publication window and the vertical ruler is displayed down the left side
Sans serif	A style of font which does not have short lines or curves (serifs) attached to its characters
Scaling	To increase or decrease the size of an image file within a frame
Serif	A style of font which has short lines or curves (serifs) attached to the vertical lines of its characters
Story Editor	PageMakers built-in word processor
Style sheet	The master page and paragraph styles for a given document
Tag	A format that applies to a particular paragraph or paragraphs
Template	A model page that incorporates column guides and styles
Text block	A variable amount of text (identified by two types of handles when selected with the pointer tool in PageMaker)
Thumbnail	A miniature image of a page
TIFF	Acronym for Tagged Image File Format which is an industry standard file format for pictures
Tint	The underlying shade or pattern inside a frame

Typeface	The appearance and style of type
Typesetting	The act of putting text into a font and column width
Widow	The last line of a paragraph situated at the top of a column or page, separated from the bulk of the paragraph in the preceding column or page
Window	A frame on screen used for dialogue with the application software or in which another function separate from the current function can be carried out
WYSIWYG	Acronym for What You See Is What You Get. It refers to the ability to show on screen an accurate representation of what will be printed out